# No Dream Is Too High

# No Dream Is Too High

## Life Lessons From a Man Who Walked on the Moon

# BUZZ ALDRIN

With Ken Abraham

**NATIONAL GEOGRAPHIC**

Washington, D.C.

Published by National Geographic Partners, LLC

The quoted comment from Ed White on page 51 is reprinted from Virgil "Gus" Grissom, *Gemini!: A Personal Account of Man's Venture Into Space* (New York: The Macmillan Company, 1968), p. 78.

The passage from the speech President Nixon prepared in case the Apollo 11 mission failed on pages 100-101 is reprinted from William Safire, *Before the Fall: An Inside View of the Pre-Watergate White House* (New York: Doubleday, 2005). The actual speech is preserved in the National Archives in Washington, D.C.

Library of Congress Cataloging-in-Publication Data

Names: Aldrin, Buzz. | Abraham, Ken.
Title: No dream is too high : life lessons from a man who walked on the Moon
  / Buzz Aldrin with Ken Abraham.
Description: Washington, D.C. : National Geographic, 2016.
Identifiers: LCCN 2015037069 | ISBN 9781426216497 (hardback)
Subjects: LCSH: Aldrin, Buzz. | Aldrin, Buzz--Philosophy. | Conduct of
  life--Philosophy. | Astronauts--United States--Biography. | BISAC:
  BIOGRAPHY & AUTOBIOGRAPHY / Science & Technology. | REFERENCE / Personal &
Practical Guides. | SELF-HELP / Personal Growth / General.
Classification: LCC TL789.85.A4 A3 2016 | DDC 650.1--dc23
LC record available at http://lccn.loc.gov/2015037069

National Geographic Partners, LLC
1145 17th Street NW
Washington, DC 20036-4688 USA

Become a member of National Geographic and activate your benefits today at natgeo.com/jointoday.

For information about special discounts for bulk purchases, please contact National Geographic Books Special Sales: ngspecsales@ngs.org

For rights or permissions inquiries, please contact National Geographic Books Subsidiary Rights: ngbookrights@ngs.org

Interior design: Nicole Miller

Printed in the United States of America

16/QGF-RRDML/1

*I dedicate this book to the dreamers,*
*the out-of-the-box thinkers and seat-of-the-pants innovators*
*like me: John Houbolt, Hubert Davis, Dick Battin,*
*Charlie Bassett, Ed White, and Stephen Hawking.*


*But I dedicate this especially to my dear friends and Apollo 11*
*crewmates, Neil Armstrong and Michael Collins.*

# CONTENTS

# COUNTDOWN

**B**uzz Aldrin is one of the most brilliant men I have ever met. Is he outspoken and opinionated? Oh, yes. Is he quirky? Oh, yeah. Is he eccentric at times? More than you can imagine!

But Buzz Aldrin is also one of the kindest men I have ever met. He has a heart that goes from here to the Moon and back. He is elegant and charming. He is a gentle man, generous to a fault, self-effacing, and intensely patriotic. He can be mildly irreverent, and he is one of the funniest people ever to walk on Earth or on the Moon.

Many people know Buzz from Apollo 11; others know him from his passionate speeches motivating the next generation of explorers to get their asses to Mars. Some people don't understand him when he speaks, but I know him well enough to be able to fill in the blanks.

Some of the stories he is about to share, I've heard him tell many times; others are brand new, even to me. In the pages ahead, I'm excited for you to meet the Buzz Aldrin that I know. He has so much to share with us. He really does dream big . . . and for Buzz, dreams do come true!

*Christina Korp*
*Manager and Mission Control Director to Dr. Buzz Aldrin*

# CHAPTER ONE

# THE SKY IS *NOT* THE LIMIT ... THERE ARE FOOTPRINTS ON THE MOON!

When I was a boy, some people regarded the statement "The sky is the limit" as a positive affirmation, implying that anything is possible. The truth is, the sky is *not* the limit. Nowadays, we can go much farther, and dream much higher than the sky.

I know the sky is not the limit, because there are footprints on the Moon—and I made some of them! So don't allow anyone to denigrate or inhibit your lofty aspirations. Your dreams can take you much higher and much farther than anyone ever thought possible! Mine certainly did.

For years, men and women dreamed of reaching space—exploring the Moon, other planets, and even the stars. But it wasn't until the 20th century that human beings experienced their first powered flight. In 1903, on a windy morning on Kill Devil Hills at Kitty Hawk, North Carolina, two young risk-takers, Orville and Wilbur Wright, took to the air, defying gravity in their appropriately named plane, *Flyer*.

My mother, Marion Moon—yes, that was her real maiden name—was born that same year. A mere 66 years later, Neil Armstrong and I set foot on the Moon, fulfilling the dreams of millions of people and far surpassing the expectations of those who claimed that the sky is the limit!

Nowadays, when I speak to young audiences, they are often surprised to learn that the United States was not the pioneer nation regarding space exploration. In October 1957, while I was still serving in the U.S. Air Force and stationed in Germany, the Soviet Union pulled off an unexpected technological feat. They launched Sputnik 1, a spherical, polished-metal artificial satellite with four transmitting radio antennas. The satellite emitted an odd *beep-beep* sound that could be heard on radio frequencies in the United States and elsewhere as the weird object orbited the Earth, passing several times directly over major cities in the United States. Although Sputnik's batteries ran out of power after only 21 days and the satellite eventually fell from orbit and was completely burned up as it reentered Earth's atmosphere, the Russians had led the way into space.

A year later, America formed the National Aeronautics and Space Administration—NASA—with the goal of reaching space. The space age was born, and a "space race" between Russia and the United States began, with each nation pouring millions of dollars and thousands of man-hours into besting each other's efforts. The term "space race" may have been a euphemism for the two nations' competitiveness, but the tension was real. Following World War II, the United States and the Soviet Union had emerged as the world's two great superpowers, both armed with nuclear weapons, facing off against each other in increasingly chilled relationships that came to be known as the cold war, with both nations suspicious of the other's motives.

That's why the world shuddered on April 12, 1961, when the Soviets achieved an incredible advantage by sending the first human into space, cosmonaut Yuri Gagarin, who flew in a spacecraft for one full orbit around the Earth.

The United States responded a few weeks later by launching America's first "Project Mercury" astronaut, Alan Shepard, on a 15-minute, 115-mile-high, suborbital flight that touched the edge of space.

This was definitely impressive, and most Americans wondered, *What could possibly be next?*

(

PRESIDENT JOHN F. KENNEDY WANTED an answer to that question as well, so he asked NASA and its ranks of engineers and rocket scientists, led by the brilliant Wernher von Braun, what was possible. They informed him that it would take *at least* 15 years before we could put a man on the Moon. It is a little known fact—one that I learned only recently—that Kennedy did not initially want the United States to go to the Moon. He wanted U.S. astronauts to go straight to Mars! NASA's leaders gulped hard and admitted to the president that Mars was out of reach, but the Moon might be possible within 15 years.

Rather than accepting what was "possible," on May 25, 1961, just three weeks after Alan Shepard's virginal flight, President Kennedy boldly challenged America to commit to the goal of landing a man on the Moon before the end of the decade! Many thought the challenge was impossible to meet. We had not yet even put a man into orbit. The rockets and spacecraft that we needed to go *beyond* Earth's orbit didn't exist. We didn't have the know-how.

But we *did* have a leader with a vision—including the determination, courage, and confidence that we could get there. Even when the NASA chief later informed the president that it was going to cost twice the amount of their initial projections, the president stuck with his commitment. By publicly stating our goal and by putting a time period on a specific accomplishment, President Kennedy gave us no way out. We either *had* to do it or fail, and no one was interested in failing, especially with the Russians already peering over our shoulders from their spacecraft.

When I first heard about America's space program from my friend and fellow fighter pilot Ed White, who had signed on with NASA, I was excited. If space was going to be our next new frontier, I wanted to be a part of getting there. So after I completed my tour of duty in Germany, I continued my education and received my doctorate in astronautics from the Massachusetts Institute of Technology (MIT). For my thesis, I adapted my experience as a fighter pilot during the Korean War, where I had focused on intercepting enemy aircraft, and devised a technique for two manned spacecraft to meet in space, a procedure called manned orbital rendezvous. Little did anyone—including me—know how critical this work would later be to our successfully landing on the Moon.

The first time I applied to be an astronaut, NASA turned me down. I was not a test pilot, they said, and at that time, NASA wanted *only* test pilots. Other people, no matter how bright or how talented, need not apply. Sure, I was disappointed, but I was determined and I knew the sky was not the limit, so I applied again.

This time, my jet fighter experience and NASA's interest in my concepts for space rendezvous influenced them to accept me in the third group of astronauts, eight men drawn from more than 6,000 applicants.

My MIT rendezvous studies really paid off. I knew that the critical key to our success would be our ability to separate the lunar landing module from a launch-and-reentry "mother ship," a command module, land it on the Moon's surface, then lift off and reliably rendezvous the two spacecraft in orbit around the Moon, a risky maneuver. If it failed, there would be no way to rescue the astronauts who had landed. Luckily, my MIT work was exactly what was needed to help figure out these complicated rejoining procedures. I thought about space rendezvous; talked about space rendezvous; ate, slept, and *dreamed* about space rendezvous so much that I became known to my astronaut peers as "Dr. Rendezvous."

Mercury was the first phase in the American space efforts, followed by the Gemini program, which helped us refine our skills and maintained the nation's fascination with space travel while the rockets were being developed for Apollo, the program that we hoped would take us to the Moon. Gemini was an integral part of our training, as it helped us learn to spacewalk. As an avid scuba diver, I was the first astronaut to train underwater to simulate weightlessness in space. Although not identical to the sensations in space, practicing movements underwater in neutral buoyancy and attempting to maneuver while wearing a bulky backpack gave me great confidence and helped me to overcome the challenges I thought I might experience once outside the space capsule.

During my first spaceflight as pilot of Gemini 12, I set a world record for spacewalking—which was actually more of a space *float*, rather than a five and a half hours' "walk" in space—tethered to the spacecraft by a single, long umbilical cord that provided life support, while circling the globe every 90 minutes at a speed of 17,500 miles an hour. Because there is no air in space, there was no resistance, so the spacecraft and I drifted along at the same tremendous speed. What a sight to behold the Earth below while floating *outside* our spacecraft! It was such a fabulous ride, I only reluctantly climbed back inside our Gemini 12 spacecraft when it was time to come home, but not before I pulled a prank on Jim Lovell.

Most people know that astronauts are competitive with each other, even those working together as crewmates, as were Jim Lovell and I on Gemini 12. Knowing that I was scheduled to perform a space walk during our flight, I had packed a banner reading "BEAT NAVY" among my personal items. I was a West Point grad, and an Air Force fighter pilot, and Jim was a Navy guy. So while I was outside doing my space walk, I took the banner with me and unfurled it, holding it up to the Gemini 12 window so Jim would have to read "Beat Navy." I still have that banner to this day, not to mention a hefty dose of competition with the Navy and with Jim!

During the same space walk, I took what would become known as the first "selfie" in space! But I'll tell you more about that later.

After nearly four days in orbit, Jim Lovell and I returned to Earth, having completed the final mission in the Gemini program. It was November 1966, and we had only three years remaining to accomplish President Kennedy's challenge to land a man on the Moon by the end of the decade. Gemini had prepared us for the Apollo missions to the Moon, but we still had a lot of work to do.

Neil Armstrong, Michael Collins, and I were chosen as the crew for Apollo 11, which would turn out to be a uniquely historic mission. Neil and I had worked together as the backup crew for Apollo 8, the first mission to reach the Moon, although not landing on the surface. Mike was originally part of the Apollo 8 crew, but due to back surgery, he had to be replaced, and he missed the opportunity. A great guy, a hard worker, and a real team player with a quick sense of humor, Mike had studied and trained diligently for Apollo 8, so I was not surprised when Neil chose Mike for our crew. He was an excellent choice.

For six months, we worked every day and prepared as best we could for this fascinating trip into the unknown. At last, the day came when the enormous Saturn V rocket was rolled out from the huge Vehicle Assembly Building, inching along on a giant transport platform, slowly making its way to the launchpad.

On July 16, 1969, our launch day, at 9:32 a.m. the engines ignited and roared with more than 7 million pounds of thrust, lifting 3,000 tons of spacecraft, fuel, equipment, and, oh yes—three very fortunate human astronauts on their way to another celestial body.

As we cleared the gantry and rocketed skyward, we were pressed into our seats as the rapid acceleration of the rocket increased our body weight. Within three minutes, we were 45 miles high, experiencing 3½ g's—the force making our bodies feel increasingly heavier than on Earth—and accelerating to nearly 6,500 miles an hour. A minute later, we passed through the 62-mile threshold, where the blue sky turns to the blackness of space. By 12 minutes after launch, we were traveling at more than 17,000 miles an hour, the speed required for us to orbit the Earth. For the next three hours, we circled around our home planet and ran through checklists to make sure that everything in our spacecraft was working properly. Then we fired the rocket engine that accelerated us to 25,000 miles an hour on a trajectory bound for the Moon.

During the eight-day round-trip journey, Mike, Neil, and I lived in a space capsule about the size of a standard automobile interior—a small vehicle not much larger than a Volkswagen van. If all went as planned, Neil and I would spend a portion of that time landing on and exploring a small part of the lunar surface.

(

ON DAY THREE, WE FIRED OUR ENGINE to slow us down enough for the Moon's gravity to capture us and draw us into lunar orbit. Another engine burn put us in the right orbit for a landing.

Thirteen orbits of the Moon later, on the morning of Sunday, July 20, 1969, Neil and I entered the lunar landing craft we had named the *Eagle*. We carefully separated our new home from the command module, *Columbia*, where Mike remained. Piloting our powered descent to the Moon's Sea of Tranquility was the most complicated and critical aspect of the whole mission. Landing was the hard part.

As we descended, we saw that our planned landing site was filled with large boulders surrounding a crater that Neil estimated to be more than a hundred feet wide, with steep slopes, so we continued maneuvering the *Eagle,* hoping to find a safe area on which to land. This unexpected extension of our trip expended additional fuel, so after traveling 240,000 miles to reach the Moon's surface, we were dangerously low on fuel and within seconds of having to either abort the mission or crash onto the lunar surface. Hovering above the Moon's surface like a slow-moving helicopter, Neil finally spied what appeared to be a safe landing spot. When we finally touched down, we had only 15 to 20 seconds of fuel remaining!

Neil and I breathed a little easier but we couldn't relax. We shook hands—we had done it; we had landed on the Moon! But this was no time for a victory party; we quickly went through our flight checklist. It was absolutely essential that we not allow our emotions to overwhelm us or cloud our thinking as we followed our planned procedures in case we had to make a hasty departure from the Moon, using an entirely different rocket engine from the one we'd used for our descent. Finally, I paused long enough to glance out the window at the black velvet sky and the ash gray, pockmarked terrain on which we had landed. With our engines shut down, we were surrounded by a celestial silence; the only sound I could hear was my own breathing.

Giving voice to a surprise that only he; Mike; our fellow astronaut Charlie Duke, who was serving as our spacecraft or capsule communicator (CAPCOM); and I knew about, Neil spoke the words "Houston, Tranquility Base here. The *Eagle* has landed." Nobody else on Earth knew that we were going to call our little portion of the Moon "Tranquility Base," and even Charlie seemed slightly caught off guard.

"Roger, Twan . . ." he started to mispronounce the name, and then corrected himself. "Tranquility."

Although few people were familiar with Tranquility Base, everyone in the world understood the significance of the latter part of Neil's calm declaration. "The *Eagle* has landed." Human beings were on the Moon!

(

ONE OF MY ASSIGNMENTS while on the surface was to literally kick up some Moon dust and observe the dust's "scuff/cohesion/adhesion" qualities. Because there is no air on the Moon, and only one-sixth of the gravity we are accustomed to on Earth, each kick of my boot sent Moon dust spraying out from my boot and falling back to the surface in perfect little semicircles, appearing almost like a handheld fan.

I was intrigued by the Moon dust, so while Neil was collecting rock samples, I borrowed the camera. I looked around the lunar surface for an undisturbed area where we had not walked so I could take a shot of a footprint. I found a good location and took a picture of the gray surface. Then I carefully pressed my foot down right in the center of the flat area I had photographed—sort of a "before" and an "after" shot. Barring obliteration by an asteroid or future human disturbance, I realized that the single, solitary footprint showing impressions made by the treads of my boot would remain intact on the lunar surface for thousands of years, convincing future explorers that man had indeed walked on the Moon.

But the more I looked at the footprint, it struck me, *Hmm, that isolated print is rather lonely looking.* So I had another idea. *I'm going to put my foot down on the surface and then pull my boot up and away from the footprint, but only slightly, still keeping my boot in the frame.*

The resulting photograph of my foot and footprint on the Moon became another famous piece of history, a symbol of human beings' passion to explore, and a powerful reminder that the sky is not the limit, because there are footprints on the Moon. Those bootprint photos are among the few that I took while on the Moon.

When Neil and I got back in the *Eagle,* we took off our heavy backpacks, and along with other unnecessary items such as our boots and our specially designed, 70-millimeter Hasselblad camera, we placed them in garbage bags and tossed them out on the lunar surface. Those items are still on the Moon today. In retrospect, we probably should have tossed out our helmets rather than the boots—that might have had more historic significance—and the Hasselblad camera; the helmets were much heavier, but there was always the possibility that we might still need them. Perhaps future space environmentalists will find our castoffs and criticize us for so inconsiderately discarding our "trash," but we dared not take off with one ounce more than planned, and we had already picked up some weight with the more than 45 pounds of rocks we had gathered on the Moon to take back to Earth for study.

We left a commemorative plaque on the lunar surface. Dated July 1969, the plaque depicts the two hemispheres of the Earth and reads: "HERE MEN FROM THE PLANET EARTH FIRST SET FOOT UPON THE MOON. WE CAME IN PEACE FOR ALL MANKIND."

☾

I'VE LEARNED MUCH ABOUT MYSELF since the *Eagle* whisked Neil and me off the lunar surface all those years ago. I've experienced my share of ups and downs, some successes and failures; I've met a lot of interesting people, and I've had a lot of fun. Some of the lessons I've learned have been painful; others have been hilarious. All have helped shape me and have served me well. I know the lessons I will share with you in this book *work,* because I have tested them for more than 86 years. They have worked for me, and I believe that if you will adapt them to your circumstances, they will serve you well, too.

One truth I have discovered for sure: When you believe that all things are possible and you are willing to work hard to accomplish your goals, you *can* achieve the next "impossible" dream. No dream is too high!

# CHAPTER TWO

# KEEP YOUR MIND OPEN
# TO POSSIBILITIES.

I've often said, "Your mind is like a parachute: If it isn't open, it doesn't work."

Innovators and explorers like to ponder what might be possible, not merely what is expected. That's why I try to stay open to new ideas. I'm constantly dreaming up new things, sketching new rocket designs, and looking for new areas to explore.

"Innovation" is my middle name . . . unless I decide to change it to "Lightyear." In fact, one of the awards of which I am most proud is the Lifetime Innovation Achievement Award I received in 2015 from New Jersey, the state where I lived as a boy.

Speaking of my name, people often ask me, "Colonel Aldrin, is Buzz your real name?"

The answer is yes. Although my parents named me Edwin Eugene Aldrin, Jr., when I was born, Fay Ann, my two-year-old sister, had difficulty pronouncing "brother," so she called me "Buzzer." No doubt, over the years, a few people have called me "Buzzard," but from the time I was a baby, the name Buzz has been a part of my life. Years later, after Apollo 11, and after my father, for whom I had been named, passed away, I legally changed my name simply for the convenience and clarity. But although Buzz is now my real legal name, innovation is my guiding spirit. I've always been quick to try new ideas, especially new ways of doing things in space.

During the early years of space exploration, a number of the initial Russian cosmonauts and American astronauts had experienced nausea during their first trips into space. Their bodies simply weren't accustomed to the unusual sensations and disorientation brought on by trying to move and work in a weightless environment. In preparation for my Gemini 12 space walk, I welcomed the opportunity to become the first astronaut trained underwater in a swimming pool to simulate the effects of neutral buoyancy, trying to maneuver in a weightless environment in space. Some of my colleagues thought I was being eccentric, but the sensations in the pool prepared me for what it might feel like drifting along at 17,500 miles an hour, tethered to a spacecraft.

Ironically, in space exploration, as in business or any other area of life, past success can be the greatest obstacle to future innovation. Even wonderfully brilliant people can become entrenched in the status quo, stuck in the usual way of doing things. One of the greatest impediments to discovery is the attitude that says, "We don't do things that way," or its counterpart, "We've never done things that way." Which basically means, "I don't want to change."

So we've never done it that way before? Great! Let's try something new; let's come up with a different approach, another way of reaching our goals. You have to stay open to the possibilities. Remember, your mind is like a parachute: If it isn't open, it doesn't work. So keep an open mind!

It was a man with an open mind who made it physically possible for human beings to land on the Moon. Many people have never heard of him, but John Houbolt was the man who may have saved the space program.

During the early days of television and motion pictures, it was not uncommon to see a science fiction movie depicting an enormous spacecraft blasting off from Earth and landing on the Moon. That single spacecraft idea had become so embedded in people's minds, rarely did anyone question how in the world we were going to send a massive rocket like that to the Moon, land on the surface, explore, then blast off again and return to Earth, where we'd need another safe landing. Even scientists were baffled, scratching their heads in frustration because everyone thought in terms of only one gigantic spacecraft.

Everyone, that is, except John Houbolt, a bright, clever NASA engineer. John came up with the concept of using two specialized spacecraft—a command/service module and a lunar landing module—rather than one heavy spaceship in our efforts to get to the Moon, land on the surface, and get back home. The command module would stay in orbit around the Moon while the lunar landing module would be equipped with a "descent" stage that could be left on the surface, as well as an "ascent" stage with its own engine for blasting off the Moon and then rendezvousing with the command module. This was especially important because the lunar lander's rocket motors did not have to be nearly so large, since they would be needed only to power the ascent section until it rendezvoused with the command module for the return trip back to Earth.

It was a novel idea, and many people at NASA questioned John's "fanciful notions," but they finally realized the advantages of having two spacecraft rather than one huge one. John's willingness to keep his mind open and to think creatively opened the door to whole new vistas of space exploration.

Another brilliant, open-minded engineer who worked with us on the Apollo program was Hubert (Hu) Davis. Although the astronauts training for a potential landing on the Moon might not have realized it early on, the lunar landing modules (LMs) were too heavy to safely land. Hubert Davis was the project manager for LM-5, and when he heard about the problem and that his spacecraft was not slated to land, he said to NASA, "We'll work to reduce the weight, if you will consider putting LM-5 as the first lander." Hu and his team went back to work. They tried everything they knew to do.

After five versions of the LM (LM-1 to LM-5), it was still too heavy. Hubert didn't say, "Well, that's too bad; that's what the lander has to be, so deal with it." No, just the opposite. Hubert Davis put his mind to work on every way possible to reduce the weight load of the lunar lander, considering everything from the metallic materials used on the outside "skin" of the lander to how many pens Neil and I carried aboard the spacecraft. Every ounce mattered.

When almost everyone said it was impossible, Hubert Davis found a way to lighten the weight of the LM, making it possible for LM-5 to land on the Moon. Because of Hu's imaginative thinking, NASA began offering financial bonuses to aerospace companies and contractors who could reduce the weight of the LMs in production. Had Hu not found a way, Neil and I would not have attempted a landing during Apollo 11, and NASA would have been forced to wait for LM-6 and Apollo 12—or possibly even later—to land. So in a very real way, Hubert Davis made it possible for Neil and me to land on the Moon. Why? Because Hubert Davis kept his mind open to the possibilities.

$$\left($$

INNOVATORS ARE OFTEN OUT OF SYNC with many people around them. No doubt about it—from Leonardo da Vinci to my friend Sir Richard Branson, owner of Virgin Galactic—some of history's most creative people have been a bit quirky. Anyone who saw Albert Einstein trudging along the sidewalks of Princeton University with a briar pipe hanging out of his mouth might have assumed the odd fellow in the old, frumpy overcoat and socks that didn't match was a hobo. Today, students at Princeton are still studying Einstein's formulas and ideas, and his adage "Subtle is the Lord, but malicious He is not" is inscribed in the stone mantel of the fireplace in the mathematics building on campus. I guess I used many of Einstein's ideas when I developed my own mathematical equations regarding space rendezvous.

Because of my fascination with rendezvous principles necessary for the lunar module to lift off the Moon's surface and be reunited with the command module, some of my fellow astronauts thought I was obsessed with the subject. They called me "Dr. Rendezvous," usually with respect, but sometimes with a hint of derision as well. I didn't care; I knew I was a little out of sync with my buddies, but that was okay. I was doing what I loved.

Sometimes innovators come across as arrogant, stubborn, or unreasonable. I'm sorry to say that I probably did, too, while working as an astronaut. Think of people such as Elon Musk, the driving force behind SpaceX, the company upon whom America is currently relying to deliver supplies and equipment to the International Space Station. Or think of Jeff Bezos, who founded Amazon.com, or Steve Jobs, the whiz behind Apple's success. As young men, they were out of sync with many of their peers; they saw things differently, wanted to do things differently. They refused to simply accept the "usual" way. Rather than seeing the world with a "that's just the way things are" attitude, they developed an intense, indefatigable desire to improve the world by radically changing the way things could be done. We relish their successes today, acknowledging that these innovators and others like them have changed our world to fit their vision of how life can be better.

Average people tend to think about merely maintaining the status quo; unsuccessful people think about simply surviving. Innovators and explorers think about what might be possible.

☾

PARENTS AND EDUCATORS OFTEN ASK me, "Buzz, how can we help foster the sort of innovation that took you to the Moon?"

First and foremost, it is important to understand that whether by nature or nurture, innovators approach the world differently. Keeping that in mind might help you to regard your boss with greater respect, or your artist friend, or the kid who wants to sit around playing his guitar all day long. Certainly, some people are born with innovation in their veins. I think I was. My father loved flying and exposed me to the possibilities of flight early in my life, but something inside me responded far beyond what my father might have imagined.

I also think that innovation can be encouraged when parents and educators understand that innovators often do not fit "the norm." Innovators whose minds are open tend to have personality traits that others might regard as quirky or sometimes even "weird." They are dreamers, and I am definitely one of them, so I know that innovators are rarely content merely to dream. They won't stop there—especially if they receive some encouragement. They will become *doers;* they will make things happen. Innovators are usually much more self-confident than their peers; they are inner directed and willing to march to the beat of their own drums. But it sure helps having someone lay a hand on a shoulder or look the innovator in the eye and say, "I believe in you; you can do it."

Often innovators are courageous and resilient, sometimes because they have had to develop such qualities in the face of adversity or opposition to their ideas. Almost always, they are risktakers, willing to try something new.

So understanding that the innovator's personality causes him or her to be out of sync with others is tremendously important, especially when it comes to encouraging exploration of new concepts or new ways of doing things.

Second, it is important to understand that innovation usually takes time. Great ideas rarely move from the mind to the Moon, or to the marketplace, overnight. They need time to percolate, to improve, to develop. At NASA, we were constantly working to make improvements on our spacecraft, as well as ourselves, as we pursued our goals. Innovators need a place to do that, and in most cases, nowadays, great innovation necessitates somebody providing a physical place and the financial resources that allow creativity to thrive. Personally, I love living at the beach; the environment itself helps stimulate my thinking. For me, dull, drab, gray walls are not normally conducive to my creativity. But whatever your preferences, recognize that your physical space will be an important component in stifling or fostering your creative juices. Even if you live in a small, one-room apartment, create a space around you where creativity can thrive.

Innovators must be encouraged to experiment with new ideas, new ways of doing things. Rather than being punished for mistakes or failures, they should be applauded for attempting to go where human beings have never gone before. That means innovators must be given the freedom to challenge the status quo. Certainly, this requires a great deal of patience and trust on the part of parents, educators, and CEOs, but as you look around our society, businesses as well as scientific cultures that encourage innovation are thriving. Companies such as Google and Apple have created a culture that empowers their employees to stretch, to attempt the "impossible dream," to explore, to go after opportunities that may not always work out.

Third, to encourage innovation, we must model and communicate that "thinking" is not wasted time but is integral to the innovation process. Unfortunately, most educators and almost all employers expect thinking to be done on a person's own time, not on the clock. Imagine you are sitting at your desk, ruminating about an idea, when your boss comes along. What's the first thing most of us do? We try to "look busy."

Allowing a person time and freedom to peer off into space, to daydream if you will, about an idea's potential is not permitting that person to be idle or unproductive. It is allowing him or her to think creatively. Allowing for the thinking process to develop in a person's mind is essential if we ever expect that individual to provide us with those *voilà!* moments. People who achieve the great breakthroughs in our world have usually already experienced those breakthroughs in their mental processing; they've seen the idea working in their mind long before they ever tried it in "real life." Before I ever took my first walk in space, I saw it in my mind many times, imagining what it might look like, feel like, sound like—all in my mind. If we want to foster innovation, we must encourage an atmosphere that allows for creative thinking, even if, to some people who may not understand, it looks as though nothing tangible is being done or accomplished.

Innovators view change as an opportunity rather than an inconvenience or an interruption. At 86 years of age, I decided to move from Los Angeles back to near Cape Canaveral in Florida. Sure, it is challenging to deal with change, but I always want to be open to new opportunities. Most people don't like to move out of their comfort zones, but as we all know, change is inevitable. You can resist it and complain about it as an inconvenience, or you can regard change as your chance to do something new. Keep that parachute open. Use your mind to ponder the possibilities rather than to pooh-pooh the interruptions change brings to your "normal" way of doing things.

Albert von Szent-Györgyi, the Hungarian Nobel Prize–winning physiologist who first discovered the benefits of vitamin C, was fond of saying, "Discovery lies in seeing what everyone sees, but thinking what no one else has thought."

That was a man who kept his mind open to the possibilities, and that's the kind of man I have tried to be, and always want to be.

# CHAPTER THREE

# SHOW ME YOUR FRIENDS, AND I WILL SHOW YOU YOUR FUTURE.

Choose your heroes wisely, and be careful who you idolize. Why? Simple: You will become like the people with whom you most often associate. The people with whom you surround yourself will have an impact on you, either positively or negatively. It is a timeless truth that bad company corrupts good character, but if you walk with the wise, you will become more like them.

I've been blessed with some great friends, people who have not only given of themselves to help me, but who have helped to bring out the best in me. Other than my father, one person who was a great friend to me, as well as my most influential mentor, was Jimmy Doolittle, the famous aviator. When my dad introduced me to Doolittle, I was just a kid, but the world-renowned pilot took time with me and encouraged me to pursue my own dreams of flying.

When my father passed away, Jimmy Doolittle, more than any other person, encouraged me and helped me to deal with my dad's death, and to keep moving forward with my own life.

Another of the places where I experienced that sort of friendship and camaraderie was in the Air Force.

A year before I graduated from West Point, I went along with my fellow cadets on a social science tour of the Far East, studying General Douglas MacArthur's occupation of Japan. When I awakened after my first night in Tokyo, the newspaper headlines read: "**NORTH KOREA ATTACKS SOUTH KOREA.**"

To the world's surprise, 75,000 North Korean soldiers had poured across the 38th parallel, the boundary between the Soviet-backed Democratic People's Republic of Korea to the north and the pro-Western Republic of Korea to the south. As an ally of the United States, South Korea sought our help, and the United States was determined to come to the aid of our friend. As far as Americans were concerned, North Korea's unprovoked attack against South Korea was an example of communist aggression, and many people felt certain that the communists would not stop at Korea, that this was a blatant step toward communist world domination.

Consequently, by July 1950, American troops entered the war on South Korea's behalf. Although I still had another year to go at West Point, I knew that if the war continued, I would soon be fighting in Korea.

My father had urged me to attend the Naval Academy—"You can still fly in the Navy," he said, but my friends and I wanted to be where the action was—and that was in the skies above Korea. Of course, my natural interest in aviation nudged me more toward enlisting in what had until recently been known as the Army Air Corps and eventually became a separate branch of the military, the U.S. Air Force.

By the end of the summer, U.S.-led allies pushed the North Koreans out of Seoul and back to their side of the 38th parallel. But as American troops crossed the boundary and headed north toward the Yalu River, the border between North Korea and communist China, the Chinese started squawking about what they called "armed aggression against Chinese territory." Chinese leader Mao Zedong even sent troops to North Korea and warned the United States to keep away from the Yalu boundary unless we wanted to engage *them* in a full-scale war. With China threatening to get involved and images of World War II still fresh in our minds, many people worried that we were getting dangerously close to World War III.

I graduated number three in my class at West Point, and by December 1952, even though negotiators were trying to bring the war to a close, I put in for combat duty stationed in Korea. I had already earned my wings and qualified as a pilot of the Sabre F-86; I soloed in prop T-6's at Bartow Air Force Base in Florida and then flew jets at Bryan Air Force Base in Texas, so I sure didn't want a desk job!

Flying the Sabre F-86 swept-wing fighter jet and chasing the enemy's superagile, Soviet-made MiG-15 jets were some of the most exciting moments of my life. I flew 66 missions over the war zone, had a few close calls, and I shot down two enemy MiGs.

The MiGs could fly higher and faster than our fighter jets, and they carried a vicious 37-millimeter cannon and two 23-millimeter automatics that could shred an F-86 with one burst of fire. But what the American-made planes lacked in altitude and speed, we more than compensated for with advanced technology, much as we would in the space race in the 1960s and 1970s.

On May 14, 1953, I was flying on patrol, hunting for enemy aircraft in the skies just south of the Yalu River. Because the North Korean ground war effort had almost disintegrated, they had moved many of their best planes as far north as possible, close to the Yalu in a location my buddies and I referred to as "MiG Alley." On a good day, it could be like picking off ducks in a shooting gallery, with "free" shots at enemy planes still on the ground. On a bad day, an F-86 pilot could experience his worst nightmare—a faster killing machine with deadly fire-power on his tail, or worse yet, two or three MiGs surrounding him in a dogfight that was certain not to last very long.

On that day in May, I was the pilot with the advantage. Flying just south of the Yalu, I spied a MiG cruising ahead of me, straight and level. Apparently, he didn't know that I was nearby or he would not have been so lackadaisical. I aimed my guns at him and fired, lighting up the MiG.

The enemy fighter jet spun hard and pitched toward the ground. The pilot, still alive, succeeded in ejecting from his cockpit, but his plane streaked toward the Earth. The camera on the gun of my F-86 recorded the whole episode, including the pilot's ejection and the plane veering toward destruction. Actually, I'm glad the pilot ejected, and I like to think that he escaped harm, even though I shot down his plane. I've always thought of myself as a "gentle" fighter pilot!

Our military public relations guys, however, loved those videos of "kills," and several photo frames from the incident appeared in the next issue of *Life* magazine, one of the premier news magazines of that time.

About a month later, I was flying a mission with three other pilots attached to the 16th "Blue Tail" Squadron, and following four other, newer Sabre jets from the 39th "Yellow Tail" Squadron. Just as we were taking off, my wingman aborted his flight, so I radioed my commander for permission to join up with the Yellow Tails. That was okay at first, but the newer F-86 Sabres were much faster than my older F-86 model, and I was having a tough time staying with them. When they dove toward a valley near the Yalu, blasting away at an enemy airfield, I couldn't keep up with them, even with my airspeed indicator pegged.

I spotted some enemy MiGs racing down the runway, hoping to get into the air, both to save their planes and to engage the Sabres. Just then, an enemy fighter jet streaked across my sight from left to right. Because I had been unable to keep up with my buddies, I was behind them, and if I could stay calm, I had a shot at the MiG. If I missed him, he'd be right on the tail of my buddies.

I tried to slow my aircraft before he saw me, but the MiG pilot spotted me and banked hard in my direction. The good news was that I had pulled him off my friends. The bad news? He was coming after *me!* Worse yet, I realized that as fast as I was flying, I was bound to sweep right into his line of fire. My only hope was a desperate, dangerous maneuver that pilots referred to as a "scissors" move, cutting across the enemy's path, with both aircraft crisscrossing back and forth, each trying to seize an advantage. We ripped through one set of scissors moves and then I banked so steeply that my wingtips pointed straight down to the ground as I raced above the enemy runway, flying sideways. I could hear enemy antiaircraft fire all around me, but I hadn't been hit. The MiG rolled off to avoid a mountainous ridge below us, and I knew this was my chance—probably my only shot.

I tried to fire, but the aiming dot on my gun sight jammed! Still flying with my left wing pointing toward the earth, I used my plane's nose as a sight and pressed hard on the trigger of my .50-caliber machine gun.

I saw something spark on the MiG, so I quickly rolled back parallel to the ground, pulled hard on the throttle, and gassed it for all the F-86 was worth. The MiG was still in front of me, and he was going into a steep right-hand turn to come back after me. I fired again and saw tracers sparking across his wing, but he was still going! We were too close to the ground for this fight to last much longer; I knew one of us was going down. The enemy rolled out of the turn and dove, so I fired two more rapid bursts from the machine guns, just as he turned up toward me.

It was like a slow-motion movie as I watched the enemy plane's nose come up and seem to hang in the air, the engine stalling. The canopy of the jet opened, and I saw the flash of the pilot's ejection flare. Whether he had time to open a parachute, I don't know, but the MiG definitely beat him to the ground.

There was no time to celebrate. I had been going so fast that I had little idea where I was, but I figured I was about 20 miles north of the Yalu, and there were more Russian and now Chinese planes as well, rising off the runway below. I turned south and hightailed it out of there as fast as I could, fortunately picking up the Manchurian Express, a jet stream that helped me fly even faster with less resistance, which was another stroke of luck, because I was running low on fuel. I had no idea where my buddies were, and as I was climbing out, I suddenly realized that I still had my speed brakes engaged. I felt like an idiot, but fortunately I was able to correct the mistake and make it back to our base.

The Air Force awarded me an Oak Leaf Cluster as well as the Distinguished Flying Cross for dropping the first MiG, and although my gun camera clearly showed that I had destroyed the second enemy plane, there was a question as to which side of the Yalu River I had been on when I shot it down. Consequently, I received no special honor for winning one of the most dangerous battles of my life. But I was thrilled that I had helped to protect my buddies and that I had taken another enemy of our nation out of the sky. As with many conflicts I'd encounter in life, it really didn't matter who got the credit. What mattered was taking care of each other.

I'm certainly not infallible, and I've had some experiences that some of my friends and colleagues might be ashamed to admit. But we all make mistakes and sometimes cross some lines that we shouldn't. A few of my mistakes almost cost me my life.

On another occasion, I almost ran out of fuel while flying close to the Chinese/North Korean border. I had to stay calm and nurse my fuel supply all the way back to base. As I've often said, fighter pilots don't have emotions; we have ice in our veins. That quality served me well when, 16 years later, the Apollo 11 computers began to malfunction, just as Neil and I closed in on landing on the Moon. I'll tell you more about that later!

(

ON ONE PATROL OVER NORTHERN KOREA, I was flying in formation with good friend and wingman Sam Johnson when we lost contact. The wingmen looked out for each other, flying side by side and watching each other's backs. Sam and I flew all the way to the Yalu River, the boundary American pilots were warned not to cross.

We saw some movement on the ground and some other things going on that we might be able to do something about, but we had no orders from our commanding officers allowing us to attack, and we were too close to the Yalu River and the Chinese border, plus I was concerned about our fuel levels. It was a dangerous situation.

I said to Sam, "It's time to head back." I looked out my cockpit window, expecting to see Sam behind me to the side, but I couldn't spot him and he didn't respond. That wasn't like Sam, so I got worried.

"Sam, where are you?" I asked. "I can't see you."

Suddenly, through the familiar sound of Sam's gunnery fire, *rat-a-tat-tat; ehh-ehh-ehh-ehh,* I heard Sam's voice on my headset. "I'll be right with you, Buzz!" More gunnery fire: *Ehh-ehhh-ehhh-ehhhh.* Clearly, Sam was engaged with the enemy somewhere in the skies nearby. I swerved my F-86 hard, turning around quickly, as my eyes searched for Sam's plane. If my buddy was in trouble, I had to help him.

Next thing I knew, Sam was flying right beside me. We chased the MiGs as far as we dared, but they were too fast for us to catch up. We zoomed out of the danger zone and headed back to South Korea, watching our fuel gauges all the way.

When we finally got back to our base and landed, we got chewed out royally by our commanding officers. I didn't mind the scolding. After all, there was no way I was going to leave my friend when he needed me most.

To me, that is one of the most important principles of life: Never leave your friends behind. Consequently, throughout my lifetime, I've tried to keep in touch with my buddies, even though it has not always been easy, because most of us have stayed quite busy. In times past, I'd burn up the telephone lines; these days, text messaging has become my preferred method of communication, a great way for me to stay connected with my friends. But don't kid yourself. Keeping in touch requires intentionality. You must consciously make the effort to stay connected with your friends, or it won't happen. You'll gradually slip away from each other, like a married couple that once loved each other but allowed the sparks of passion and the flame of love to be snuffed out.

Time goes by and we all get caught up with daily responsibilities, priorities, and the tyranny of the urgent. It is easy to get so busy that we forget about those people who have played such important roles in our lives, so every so often, I will swing back to see how my friends are doing. It doesn't take a lot to do that. Maybe a quick phone call or a text message, perhaps a letter or a card in the mail. But it is important to stay connected, because life gives none of us any guarantees. I'm proud to say that the West Point class of 1951 keeps in contact regularly. For instance, my friend and West Point classmate Jack Craigie and I have known each other since we were 18 years old. Today, with both of us past 86 years of age, we still make the effort to keep in touch.

I did my best to keep in touch with Sam Johnson, too. In 1966, while I was working on the Gemini program, Sam flew in Vietnam. During his 25th combat mission, he was shot down and was incarcerated in a North Vietnamese prisoner of war camp, a place so desolate, with such inhumane living conditions and treatment so despicable, that he later described it as "Alcatraz."

During the war, many Americans back home wore bracelets reminding us of captured soldiers wallowing in the sweltering POW pigsties in 'Nam. I wore a metal bracelet with Sam's name, rank, and serial number engraved on it, along with the date that he was shot down. It was a symbol of hope and solidarity with our troops. I wore that bracelet to the Moon and back.

Sam didn't know that I had been on Apollo 11, because he had been kept in the dark in the Vietnamese POW camp. Even when he heard the news over a crackling radio in the prison camp that human beings from America had walked on the Moon, Sam's Vietnamese captors tried to convince him that it never happened, that it was, in fact, the Russians who had landed on the Moon. Sam refused to believe what his tormenters were telling him. My good friend Sam endured seven years as a POW in Hanoi, including 42 months in solitary confinement. It wasn't until after his release from the Vietnamese POW camp that Sam learned that his former wingman buddy had walked on the Moon.

Sam served our country in the U.S. Air Force for 29 years, flying with the precision demonstration team, the Thunderbirds, as well as on combat missions in Korea and Vietnam. Later he ran for office in the Texas state legislature, and then he went on to become a multiple-term U.S. congressman, serving the third district of Texas.

After years of separation, we reconnected, and we still keep track of each other to this day. I regard Sam as one of the best friends I've ever had and one of the best men I've ever known.

You never know how people you meet today will have an impact on your future. Another friend that I first met in Korea played a significant role in my future, because of his impact on the space program. His name was John Glenn, the Mercury program astronaut who in 1962 first orbited the Earth three times, which in the early days of America's space program was a major accomplishment. John and I flew F-86 Sabre jets together in the waning days of the war, and he succeeded in shooting down three Russian MiGs near the Yalu River, one more than I did.

Regarding his initial spaceflight, John later quipped, "As I hurtled through space, one thought kept crossing my mind: Every part of this rocket was supplied by the lowest bidder." He went on to become a U.S. senator representing his home state of Ohio. While still a sitting senator, at 77 years of age, John went back into space for a nine-day mission aboard the space shuttle *Discovery*, and to date he is the oldest person ever to travel into space.

John and I still share a passion for space exploration, although neither of us could have imagined such a thing when we first met in 1953. But your friends do rub off on you.

Serving my country in Korea was a marvelous time in my life. After chasing Soviet MiGs all day, my buddies and I would gather together and tell our stories. We were intensely competitive with each other, but we also shared a special camaraderie, much like the relationships I would have with NASA astronauts a few years later. It was an experience like iron sharpening iron, similar to our time at West Point, where we brought out the best in each other. Eventually—often after a few adult beverages—someone would break into a song. We had an entire repertoire of fighter pilot songs that I still sing sometimes, even after all these years. And when I sing those songs, in my mind, I'm right back there in Korea with all those great friends.

Besides stopping the Soviet-supplied communists from North Korea in their efforts to overrun South Korea, the war also created a fringe benefit for America that often goes unnoticed. That is: Most of the early U.S. astronauts were not veterans of World War II. Most of us were fighter pilots who flew during the Korean War. In addition to the missions flown by John Glenn, Neil Armstrong flew 78 combat missions in Korea. Wally Schirra flew 90 missions; Gus Grissom flew 100 combat missions over Korea; Jim McDivitt flew 145 missions! And of course, I flew 66 missions chasing MiGs.

As fighter pilots in Korea, we learned concentration under fire, how to stay calm in the face of dangerous situations, and how to make quick, life-or-death decisions. Beyond that, because we knew that we were really fighting the Soviets as well as the North Koreans, the war spurred a passionate competition between the Americans and the Russians that would carry over into the space race. We were not going to let those "Russkies" beat us in Korea, and we were certainly not going to let them get the upper hand on us in space.

(

You never know when the next person you meet might be someone who impacts your life for the better, or someone to whom you can give a helping hand. Shortly after I moved to Houston to become part of the U.S. space program, I was visiting with my friend Ed White when we saw a guy out roller-skating on the cement behind Ed's house.

"Who is that?" I asked.

"Oh, that's Neil Armstrong, another test pilot who has been accepted for the astronaut program."

I had heard plenty of stories about Neil already—that he was a fearless test pilot with a deadpan serious personality. "That's Neil Armstrong?" I asked, watching the roller skater. He didn't look too serious to me.

I knew that Neil had been a fighter pilot in Korea as well, so we had that experience in common, and we soon struck up a long, lasting friendship, one that some people would later misunderstand and misrepresent, but a friendship that Neil and I knew was based on mutual admiration. My friendship with Neil Armstrong became another positive factor in my life. Neil and I became even better friends when we were selected to work together as the backup crew for Apollo 8. Neil was a man of few words and enjoyed being the strong, silent type. I, on the other hand, enjoyed talking about our work and the possibilities ahead. But we hit it off and had a mutual respect and appreciation for each other. We were a good team. We worked closely together almost every day for six years, and although one of us would sometimes rub the other the wrong way, we always brought out the best in each other.

Neil and I were selected as the crew for Apollo 11 in January 1969. In some ways, *because* we were selected for the first landing mission to the Moon, it created an additional strain on our friendship. We both knew there would be enormous publicity around our mission and that everything we said or did would be all over the news. When some people at NASA questioned whether I was the right man for the job, Neil came to my defense. I knew that we worked well together, and I was glad to learn that Neil felt the same way. He was quick to defend a friend, and I've always been honored to be known as his co-worker.

Not long ago, I visited Purdue University, where faculty and student researchers have been working with my Mars Cycler ideas—a system of spacecraft cycling between Earth and Mars, continually carrying people and materials in both directions. Outside the Neil Armstrong Hall of Engineering stands a large statue of Neil, who was an engineering student at Purdue in 1955. I slipped up next to the statue and cracked, "Hey, I want them to make a statue of me, sitting here beside Neil and holding his hand!"

Although all of the astronauts in training were extremely competitive, we were also friends. That made sense, because most other people couldn't really relate to our intense training, our level of commitment to the cause, and how passionately we pursued our goals of catching and passing the Russians in the exploration of space. Like any team, however, some of us clicked with each other better than others. One of the guys that I became closest to was Ed White.

Ed was a year behind me at West Point, and he and I were on the track team together and became best friends during our time at the academy. Ed enlisted in the Air Force upon his graduation in 1952. He spent three years in Germany, and he was stationed there when I arrived at Bitburg following my stint in Korea. I was stationed in Germany from 1956 to 1959, and during that time, our friendship grew even stronger.

Like me, Ed loved flying the F-86 Sabre jets as well as the incredible F-100 fighter jets in the "Big 22 Squadron" that made regular runs close to the "Iron Curtain" nations, the countries under Soviet control. We were carrying a nuclear payload, and we were ready to attack the Russians at the first sign of a nuclear threat. The Russians had already steamrolled into Budapest, crushing any opposition, so we were constantly on alert to halt any further advances by the Soviet forces in Europe. Ed and I regularly flew practice missions, loaded with bombs we were ready to deliver.

Near the end of the decade, Ed became fascinated with space. Leaving Germany, he attended the University of Michigan and earned his master's degree in aeronautical engineering the same year that NASA selected seven men as the original astronauts for Project Mercury, the first U.S.-manned space program. All seven of the initial astronauts were test pilots, so Ed enrolled in the Air Force Test Pilot School at Edwards Air Force Base in California. He was one of the pilots to fly the planes used for astronauts Deke Slayton's and John Glenn's weightless maneuvers, some of the first test flights to see how zero gravity affected humans.

As the Mercury flights concluded, NASA began recruiting a new crop of astronauts for Project Gemini. Drawing from more than 200 applicants, NASA selected Ed White and eight more test pilots: Neil Armstrong, Frank Borman, Charles Conrad, Jim Lovell, Jim McDivitt, Elliot See, Tom Stafford, and John Young. Even among this group of superachievers, Ed stood out from the crowd. Moving to Houston, like several other astronauts including me eventually, Ed and his wife, Pat, bought a home in El Lago, to be close to the Manned Space Center.

*Show Me Your Friends, and I Will Show You Your Future.*

More than any other person, Ed White was the friend who encouraged me to apply to NASA to become an astronaut.

He first went into space on the Gemini 4 mission, and on June 3, 1965, Ed was the first American astronaut to perform a successful extravehicular activity (EVA), a space walk outside the capsule for 21 minutes. A devout Methodist, Ed carried three religious reminders with him when he stepped out of the hatch—a gold cross, a Star of David, and a St. Christopher's medal. He later quipped, "I had great faith in myself, and especially in Jim [McDivitt, the mission's commander], and I think I had great faith in my God . . . The reason I took these symbols was that this was the most important thing I had going for me, and I felt that while I couldn't take one for every religion in the country, I could take the three I was most familiar with."

Besides his incredible courage, Ed had a great sense of humor. Before stepping out in space, using a handheld maneuvering gun and attached to the spacecraft by a tether, Ed checked his 35mm camera equipment three times. He said, "I wanted to make sure I didn't leave the lens cap on!"

Far too quickly, in Ed's estimation, his space walk came to an end. "I enjoyed the EVA very much, and I was sorry to see it draw to a close," he said.

Following his outstanding Gemini EVA, Ed was selected as senior pilot for Apollo 1, scheduled for launch on February 21, 1967, as America's first mission in the program that would eventually take us to the Moon. Unfortunately, as Ed, Gus Grissom, and Roger Chaffee trained and prepared, it seemed they encountered one setback after another. Finally, everything started to come together, each problem solved, so on January 27, 1967, NASA planned a "plugs out" test, a full dress rehearsal for launch, in which the Apollo 1 capsule would be unplugged from external power while the astronauts practiced emergency escape procedures.

Ed sat in the middle seat, and it was his responsibility to reach above his head with a ratchet to loosen the bolts of the hatch. The hatch door was heavy, but Ed was a strong man and in excellent physical condition. He had practiced the egress drill numerous times, although never within the 90 seconds suggested by NASA's engineers.

They started the drill around 1 p.m. and encountered more problems, including a communications microphone that would not turn off. The three astronauts were still inside the space capsule, perched atop the enormous Saturn rocket standing on Launch Pad 34, as darkness began to shroud Cape Canaveral.

It was then that something went horribly wrong. With all three astronauts buckled into their seats, and with a highly flammable, 100 percent oxygen–rich atmosphere inside the command module and flowing through their space suits, a fire broke out in the capsule. Investigators later thought the fire was caused by some sort of voltage surge or possibly an electrical short that produced a spark below the left equipment bay under Gus Grissom's seat.

Like a blowtorch, the capsule erupted in flames. Just as he had trained, Ed White struggled to open the hatch, but this time, it was not a test and the astronauts did not even have the

90-second wiggle room. Within a minute, the command module ruptured, causing an outrush of gases and creating an inferno inside the capsule, followed by deadly concentrations of carbon monoxide. The three astronauts trapped in the wall of fire never had a chance.

Ironically, none of our previous astronauts in the Mercury or Gemini programs had ever incurred a scratch, and NASA's most horrific space program accident took place not in space, but while the astronauts were still on the launchpad at Cape Canaveral. The Moon, which had seemed within reach a few hours earlier, now seemed out of sight.

Ed was my good friend and colleague; he was also a major part of my inspiration to become an astronaut. In a couple of minutes, his storied life was over. I never had a chance to thank him for all that he had meant to me, or to tell him goodbye, although two and a half years later, I carried with me to the Moon a medallion in his honor. In some way, I have tried to honor Ed by the path that I have pursued.

Life is a gift, and none of us has any guarantees about tomorrow, so don't miss the opportunity to tell your friends and family members how much they mean to you. Take the time to make that phone call just to say hello, or to write that note of encouragement.

In this day of text messages, email, and social media communications, if you really want to make an impression on someone, write a handwritten note of thanks or encouragement.

(

OVER THE YEARS, I'VE BEEN PASSIONATE about trying to reunite all of our Apollo astronauts, but it has not been easy to get everyone together. I want them to care as much as I do. Some of them may feel that they no longer have much to contribute to the space program, so they aren't as interested in talking about future exploration. On the other hand, I feel that I'm not done yet.

Apollo astronauts were friends, but it was tough to maintain a sense of normalcy, especially for the crew of Apollo 11, the first mission to land on the Moon. Most of the other guys in the Apollo program have remained close with their particular crews, but Neil, Mike, and I had a tougher time of it. At one point, Neil and I went years without seeing each other. Although we remained friends, we rarely got together socially, except at special U.S. presidential commemorations of the Apollo 11 mission, which have taken place at the White House every five years since the initial landing on the Moon.

Mike Collins and I still keep in touch, although at the beginning of every phone call, Mike is always quick to remind me, "Buzz, I don't want to talk about Mars!"

"Okay, right, Mike. But you know that scientists at Purdue University have now proven that my Mars Cycler will work . . ."

"Buzz!"

On a trip to Arizona, I was talking with Gene Cernan, commander of Apollo 17 and currently known as "the last man to walk on the Moon," about the future of space exploration, and I was getting on his case. "Gene, why are you advocating that we go back to the Moon? We don't need to be competing with other countries to go to the Moon. Don't you realize that we don't have a big budget, and we'd be wasting money, time, and energy?"

"Buzz, I don't know what you know. All I know is that I think we need to be going out farther into space."

"We've got to find a way to go beyond the Moon," I prodded him.

"I don't know anything about that, Buzz. You obviously know much more than I do. All I know is that we need to be out there."

"So you admit that you know nothing!"

Even today, when any of the Apollo astronauts get together, there is a strong sense of camaraderie mixed with a very real sense of competition. Of the 24 Apollo astronauts that reached the Moon, 12 of us actually landed on the Moon's surface. Yet, after nearly half a century, we are still competitive with each other. It's a strange brew, but we cherish our friendships, and just as iron sharpens iron, we continue to bring out the best in each other.

The late entrepreneur and motivational speaker Jim Rohn often said, "You're the average of the five people you spend the most time with." What he meant by that, of course, is that the people with whom you repeatedly choose to associate will have an enormous impact on you, either positively or negatively. That's why I say, Show me your friends and I will show you your future.

Choose friends who will bring out the best in you.

# CHAPTER FOUR

# SECOND COMES RIGHT AFTER FIRST.

☉ → ☾ → ♂

On the television show *The Simpsons,* Homer asked me how it felt to be the second man on the Moon. I told Homer, "Second comes right after first."

Who wants to be number two? You never see a team running off the field after a game, shouting, "We're number two! We're number *two!*"

No, everybody wants to be number one.

Truth is, for years, I bristled at my notoriety, being known as "the second man on the Moon." My father even made strident efforts to get the official U.S. Postal Service stamp to say "First Men on the Moon," rather than "First Man on the Moon." The Postal Service opted for "First Man."

Making matters worse, in the "normal" patterns of NASA and the space program, I *should* have been the first person to walk on the Moon. Neil was the commander, and I was the pilot. The commander normally stayed with the spacecraft while the junior officer under his command left the spacecraft to perform the EVAs. The commander had an enormous responsibility, not to mention additional training requirements, so in all previous missions, if a crew member was to spacewalk, it was always the junior officer rather than the commander. That was the way NASA had operated in every other launch prior to Apollo 11.

But NASA changed its procedures just prior to our launch. Neil, it was decided, would be the first person to set foot on the lunar surface. Once NASA decided that the mission of Apollo 11 would include an attempted landing, everything changed. We all understood that this would be different; besides being historic, two people would leave the spacecraft, not one.

When the word got out, several of my colleagues said, "This isn't right, Buzz. You should be the first one to set foot on the surface." Others, however, felt that the symbolism of the pioneer explorer arriving at his destination demanded that the commander of the mission be the first to set foot on the Moon.

Although I was excited about the possibilities of our mission, I wasn't interested in trying to manipulate opinions at NASA, or pushing to be number one. I had even expressed to my wife my misgivings about being a crew member on the first mission to the Moon, suggesting that I would rather be involved in a later trip to avoid the publicity and media frenzy and other hoopla that would most assuredly accompany the initial lunar landing. I had experienced a major dose of that sort of public spectacle after I returned to Earth following my successful space walk during Gemini 12. Although I was grateful for the many kind gestures and words expressed to me, the enormous amount of attention I received everywhere I went was overwhelming. I could barely step outside our home without being swarmed by media or fans. Nor could my mother. I'm convinced that the emotional overload following my Gemini success was a major factor in my mother committing suicide the year before I went to the Moon. That's why, given a choice, I would have preferred a later mission rather than the initial landing.

Moreover, I felt sure that later missions would focus on more experiments, and that possibility intrigued me. But Neil, Mike, and I had been the backup crew for Apollo 8, so when our rotation came up for Apollo 11, it was our turn, whether or not the mission turned out to be the first attempt at landing.

Neil took his commander responsibilities seriously. Too seriously, sometimes, for Mike and me. Mike has a great sense of humor and loves to laugh. Neil was much more serious and "dignified."

When Neil took that first "small step for man, one giant leap for mankind," he was still grasping the lunar module (LM) ladder, and his right foot remained on the LM footpad. Because scientists had no idea how deep the lunar dust might be, he tentatively placed his left foot on the surface, trying to determine if it would support his weight. It did. In fact, the LM footpads had only depressed the lunar surface about one or two inches. That was good news. Some scientists were concerned that the LM's landing pads might sink deeply into the dust, possibly tilting the LM or even toppling the landing craft on its side. But the surface held firmly. Neil's boot sank into the dust less than a quarter of an inch.

I wasn't certain what Neil would say when he first set foot on the Moon, but I was quite sure that it would not be some serendipitous statement that just popped into his mind. We were intensely aware that every move we made and every word we spoke on the Moon would be seen and heard by untold millions of people, possibly for generations to come. But I really had no idea what Neil might say the moment he first set foot on the Moon. Even as we approached the Moon, still in the command module, Mike attempted to pry the secret out of Neil, asking him questions such as, "What are you going to say when you get down there?"

"Oh, I don't know," Neil said, playing down the significance of his initial statement. "If our mission is successful, I'll think of something."

I smiled, knowing that whatever Neil decided to say, it would be well thought out and appropriate to the moment.

It was. "That's one small step for man, one giant leap for mankind," Neil proclaimed, and he was right.

About 20 minutes later, it was my turn. With Neil already on the surface and snapping photos of me, I carefully backed down the ladder and partially closed the hatch, making sure not to lock it on my way out! As I stepped onto the talcumlike lunar dust, the first words that came to mind were: *magnificent desolation*. It was a "magnificent" accomplishment for man to set foot on another world for the first time. And yet there was the "desolation" of the million-year lunar landscape with no signs of life, no atmosphere, and total blackness beyond the sunlit terrain.

Nearly a billion people all over the world watched and listened as Neil and I ventured onto the powdery lunar surface. Houston was in constant communication with us, so even though we were farther away than any two humans had ever been—except for Mike, who was circling the Moon in *Columbia*—we felt connected to home.

We spent two and a half hours on the surface—collecting rocks, setting up experiments that NASA could continue to monitor for years, and taking a few photos.

Because the camera was attached to a fitting on Neil's space suit, he took most of the photographs on the Moon, and he did an excellent job, although the photos were both a blessing and a curse. After setting up one experiment, we weren't supposed to walk in front of it, but the photos later revealed my footsteps to the right of the apparatus. Because Neil was taking the photo and there was nobody else up there, I was guilty as charged—or, as someone might say, the photo revealed "condemning evidence."

One photo that Neil took of me later became known as the "Visor Shot," one of the most famous photographs in history. At first glance, it seems like a simple picture of me standing on the rough lunar surface with the blackness of space behind me. If you look more closely at the reflection in my gold helmet visor, however, you can see the *Eagle* spacecraft, my shadow on the Moon, some of the experiments we set up, and even Neil taking the picture—all in the visor of my helmet. It is truly an astounding photograph. In one click of the camera shutter, Neil captured man's first walk on the Moon. Over the years, people have often asked me why this photo was so great. I answer with three words: Location, location, *location!*

( 

EVENTUALLY, I CAME TO EMBRACE the fact that Neil was the first man on the Moon and I was "second," and that my position was not insignificant. A relative on my mother's side of the family, Reeve Darling, and I were talking about being second, and I expressed some consternation about my dubious distinction. Reeve looked at me and said, "Buzz, you can't change history. You were the second man on the Moon. The media and everyone else focuses on the first; like in the Olympics, we want to know who won the gold medals, but we're not as interested in the silver and bronze medal winners. Accept it."

That was a turning point for me. I began to realize that although Neil would always be known as the first man on the Moon, I was there with him, and my contributions helped make Neil's first step possible. Moreover, I was a participant in and an eyewitness to that first, monumental achievement. Why should I bellyache about being second, when I had so much for which I could be thankful and excited? I am the second person in the history of human beings to set foot on another celestial body. That is a meaningful position in itself.

Oh, I do have a couple of "firsts" in space. I own the title as the first person to ever take a "selfie" in space. During my Gemini 12 space walk, I was taking photos for an experiment involving ultraviolet rays, and while outside the spacecraft, I decided to see what would happen if I took a headshot of myself with Earth over my shoulder and the vastness of space above me in the background. I was confident that I could do it because my future Apollo 11 colleague Mike Collins had taken a photo inside the space capsule during Gemini 10, but nobody had ever tried a selfie outside the spacecraft.

Nearly 50 years later, my manager and "Mission Control Director," Christina Korp, noticed that someone else had declared a photo as the first selfie in space. Christina has worked with me for a number of years, and she and her husband, Alex, along with their children Brielle and Logan, have become like family to me. Alex and Christina even named their son Logan Alexander *Buzz* Korp. The boy even has "Buzz" on his passport.

Christina not only manages my business, but she manages my life, and nowadays, she often teases that she has become my substitute mother, protecting my interests and making me behave . . . or else! We have a wonderful, close relationship, and I depend on her wisdom and expertise.

When Christina saw someone else claiming to have taken the first selfie in space, it was as though someone had insulted her family member! "Oh, I don't think so," she said, and instantly sent out the same message on Twitter. "That honor belongs to Buzz Aldrin." She pointed out the photo I had taken with the Gemini 12 infrared camera. In 2015, a collector released original, authentic NASA prints from the early days of U.S. space exploration, and a print of my selfie sold for more than $9,000 at a London auction that year. I'm not sure whose pocket that money went into, but it wasn't mine!

(

AS FAR AS I KNOW, I WAS ALSO THE FIRST person to ever relieve his bladder on the Moon, which I did immediately after jumping off the ladder of the lunar module. Neil took one small step for man and one giant leap for mankind; I took one small step for man and one giant *leak* for mankind!

In June 2012, I was in Carnarvon, Australia, a tiny town far up the western coastline, out in the middle of nowhere, where a radar station was once used to help track the Apollo missions. When I was speaking to a group of young elementary school children who asked about my first acts on the Moon, I told them a sanitized version of this story.

"Do you know what I did?" I asked the kids.

Sitting on the floor, they leaned forward and looked at me expectantly, waiting quietly for my next words.

"I peed my pants!"

The kids went crazy, elbowing each other and hooting with laughter. To think that an astronaut would do something like that! But I did.

While testing out the urine containment feature of my space suit may sound insignificant, it was actually quite a tribute to the great progress made in space technology. In earlier years, during the Mercury program, for example, when an astronaut had to "go to the bathroom," he sometimes found himself lying in a pool of his own urine.

Of course, this is one of the questions that every elementary school–aged boy wants to know: "How did you guys go to the bathroom while you were in space for all those days?"

By the time Jim Lovell and I flew on Gemini 12, NASA had become skilled in the art of waste disposal. We each used a "blue bag," with a sticky substance on it that stuck to our posteriors to collect excrement. We excreted our urine into catheters that looked something like condoms. If possible, we disposed of waste products during our extravehicular activities, which is what I did during my space walk on Gemini 12. Before rejoining Jim inside, I opened the hatch and grabbed three bags of waste products and sort of pitched them over my shoulder, straight up.

That was a mistake!

Being as familiar with orbital mechanics as I am, I should have realized what I had just done—basically launching those three bags on a free return trajectory that would eventually come straight back at us! An orbit or so later, Jim and I looked out our window, and sure enough, there they were—three bags full—and heading straight for us!

Talk about unidentified objects in space! I don't think NASA ever acknowledged that one.

( 

WHETHER NUMBER ONE, OR NUMBER TWO, or a number far down the pecking order, regardless of your position, never turn in less than your best work. Refuse to fail from lack of effort, whether physical conditioning or mental work—and don't fool yourself, *thinking* is hard work!

All work is noble, if it is legal and ethical, so do your best, whether you are first, second, or last. Never lose an opportunity, a job, an election, a competition, or anything else because you were too lazy to give it your best effort. Certainly, you need rest and recreation, but keep those in balance with hard work. Remember, while you are partying, someone else is working hard to succeed. It's okay to be second, as long as you do the absolute best you can do.

Recently, I received a special award figurine from the producers of *The Simpsons*. For my cameo "appearance" on the "second comes right after first" episode ("Deep Space Homer"), I was voted as one of the top 25 guest stars in the entire history of the show. So I guess being second is not so bad!

# CHAPTER FIVE

# WRITE YOUR OWN EPITAPH.

Some people have their epitaphs written about them after they die and some people *do* their epitaphs while they are living. By that I mean, they do something that matters; they refuse to take "no" for an answer and choose to focus on the opportunities in life rather than the obstacles. They pursue their passion rather than simply perform a function or do a job.

My passion has always been aviation. I grew up in an aviation family, and my father was an aviation pioneer. He learned to fly in 1919, and his first assignment was as an aide to General Billy Mitchell in the Philippines. Dad also knew the Wright brothers, and he even hitched a ride on the *Hindenburg* prior to its tragic accident. He met Marion Moon, the daughter of the Army Air Corps chaplain, and they soon fell in love and married. Following his stint in the Philippines, my father came home and attended the Massachusetts Institute of Technology, where he wrote his doctoral thesis on the subject of spinning airplanes. He loved to fly and spent 38 years of his life in the Army Air Corps. Shortly before I was born, he took a job as aviation fuel manager for Standard Oil Company in New Jersey.

My father was a friend of Jimmy Doolittle, another MIT graduate and an outstanding aviator and gunnery instructor in World War I. Between the two World Wars, Doolittle's fame grew even more when he continued performing aviation feats, and my father was a judge at many of those contests. During World War II, Doolittle led the first carrier-based bomber attack on mainland Japan on January 2, 1942, striking Tokyo and other strategic cities after taking off from the original Navy carrier, U.S.S. *Hornet*. A portion of his Medal of Honor citation, presented personally by President Franklin D. Roosevelt, reads: "With the apparent certainty of being forced to land in enemy territory or perish at sea, Colonel Doolittle personally led a squadron of Army bombers, manned by volunteer crews, in a highly destructive raid on the Japanese mainland." But Doolittle did not perish. In fact, Doolittle later became my primary mentor, not merely in aviation, but in life.

My father won a Piper Cub airplane in a radio station contest—yes, he actually won an airplane. That sure beats winning a couple of tickets to a rock concert anytime! I was two years old when my father took me on my first airplane ride in a red-and-white plane dubbed the *Eagle*. That first flight made an indelible impression on me. I loved being airborne in the *Eagle* and could hardly wait to fly again. Ironically, years later, when Neil Armstrong and I landed on the Moon, the lunar module in which we landed was named the *Eagle*.

All of my accomplishments in the years ahead were tucked in that airplane seat along with me as a little boy, and it has been quite a journey as the dreams and goals I had as a child have come to fruition. I'm a lucky guy, because in many ways— some planned and some experienced while rolling with the punches—I have managed to fulfill my grandest dreams, and so much more. Along the way, I've interacted with some truly extraordinary people.

I enjoy noticing some of the unusual precursors to my future success, things such as my mother's maiden name of Moon, and that my first airplane flight was in a plane dubbed the *Eagle*. Here's another: While I was at West Point, I met a guy named Winston Markey who wanted to design rockets. Winston became the valedictorian of our class. Next to his photo in my copy of our yearbook, Winston wrote, "I'll build them; you fly them!"

And he did. And I did. Winston went on to become a rocket engineer and later moved into government circles where he influenced the future of space exploration.

Coincidences? Maybe. Or maybe my course was set long before I realized. People today often think I am being modest or overly humble when I say that I was simply a guy who was at the right place at the right time, but it is true. A series of serendipitous events, many of them over which I had no control and some of them even tragic, catapulted me into position for advancement.

But even as a little boy, I loved building model airplanes and became enamored with comic books featuring fictional space travelers such as Buck Rogers and Flash Gordon. I was extremely curious and everything about aviation fascinated me.

I was 11 years old in 1941 when the Japanese attacked the United States at Pearl Harbor, so all through my early teens, I read newspapers and watched black-and-white newsreels of the various bombing campaigns in Europe and in the Pacific, studying with interest the Spitfire battles over Britain, the American planes engaged in battles against the Japanese Zeroes, and the deadly dive-bombers of the German Luftwaffe.

As an adolescent, I became interested in the mechanics of airplanes, how they functioned, and how we could make them better. When my father landed a P-38 at an airport near our home after the war, I noticed the little things; for instance, the rivets on the P-38 were not flush, as they are today on most planes. We need to improve that, I thought. Eventually, we did.

As I prepared to graduate from high school, I had several choices. My father preferred that I attend the Naval Academy, even though he had spent 38 years serving in the Army Air Corps, but I chose instead to attend West Point in 1947. I took an oath to serve my country, and that has been the guiding force in my life ever since. Not comfortable living, good-paying jobs, getting rich in the stock market, or living a life of luxury, but serving my country in the best way that I could—that has been my guiding principle.

I've had my share of setbacks and disappointments in life. When I returned from the Moon, I fell into a series of depressions and bouts with alcohol because I had great difficulty finding something meaningful to do. After you have done what no human beings have done in all of history and you know you are going to be dealing with a certain level of celebrity for the rest of your life, it is hard to get excited about a "normal" job or a mundane military career. So for a while, I experienced a roller coaster of emotions, and it wasn't until I returned to what I was passionate about—space exploration—that I truly found my equilibrium again.

I've always considered myself to be rather self-motivated and, frankly, self-sufficient. I've worked hard and achieved my goals, and I have not depended on anyone else to cut me a break or pick up my slack. One of the keys to a successful life in any field is learning to take responsibility for ourselves, rather than waiting for someone else to do something for us.

Yet there have been times in my life when my best efforts simply weren't enough, when I really needed someone to come to my aid. In those incidents, despite being a macho fighter pilot and astronaut, I learned that asking for help was not a sign of weakness, but of true strength.

One such incident came in the midst of the fabulous cross-country celebration of Apollo 11's landing on the Moon. Culminating a busy day of exuberant congratulations following our return to Earth, including ticker tape parades and celebrations in New York and Chicago, Neil, Mike, and I boarded our plane for Los Angeles, where we were to be the honored guests at a special reception hosted by President Nixon, with several thousand people and dozens of high-profile celebrities in attendance.

I was excited about the gala, but I was worried because I knew I would have to make a speech. Worse yet, I assumed that we'd speak in the order of our rank, so Neil would be first, then Mike, and I would be the last Apollo 11 astronaut to stand behind the podium. I fretted that I'd have nothing to say after my buddies had spoken.

Yes, I was one of only two human beings since the beginning of time to have walked on another celestial body. But I needed help in explaining the experience to others.

Jules Bergman, science editor for ABC News, was on board our plane to California as part of the press corps. Jules was a brilliant science reporter—not just a talking head who could read a teleprompter, but a genuine student of science. He had written numerous articles about space, and to better help him understand the program, he had even participated in some training and simulations similar to what real astronauts experience. Jules knew his stuff, so I asked him to help me put together some ideas, some talking points, and he most generously and graciously complied. I sat on the dais next to Pat Collins, Mike's wife, that evening, and I'm sure I was a terrible conversationalist, because I kept sneaking glances at the notes that Jules had written out for me to use in my speech. I've always been glad that I had the courage to ask for help, and even more grateful to Jules Bergman for helping me.

No matter who you are or how accomplished you may be, a time will come when you realize that you need help. Don't be too proud or resistant to seeking help out of fear of embarrassment, reprisal, or other consequences. Some people want to give the impression that they never have a problem in the world, that everything is wonderful in their lives. If you ask them, "How are you doing?" their first response is usually, "Fine." But oftentimes things aren't fine, and you needn't be embarrassed about finding someone who can assist you, whether the help you need is physical, financial, or emotional.

Seeking help when I was suffering with depression after returning from the Moon was a lifesaver for me—perhaps, literally. Several people in my family, including my own mother, had committed suicide, so I wondered if there was a genetic predisposition that might cause me to follow their examples. Fortunately, I found excellent doctors and friends who encouraged me and helped me to recognize that I was not trapped by the past, that I could be responsible for my own decisions, and that my emotional health was much more important than my career.

Sometimes, it is tough to admit that you need help, but it is an important step. I had always enjoyed alcohol, but when I came back from the Moon and experienced frustrations regarding the future of the space program, as well as my own future, I started drinking far too much and too often. Occasionally, I spent a few weeks in treatment centers, and although I found wonderful, short-term help, I continued a downward spiral.

For years, I struggled alone with my demons. But when I became involved in Alcoholics Anonymous, I found people who understood, who empathized, and who could also encourage me to take the necessary steps toward health and wholeness, including the willingness to keep me accountable. They helped me to discover meaning and significance and to focus on what I was good at doing. Because I was willing to ask for help, as you read these words, I have been sober for more than 36 years.

( 

I KNOW FROM EXPERIENCE just how important it is to discover and pursue a path about which you are truly excited, one that matters and is meaningful to you. If you are not sure what that is, ask yourself, "What gives me the greatest sense of joy, of meaning, of pleasure? What makes me happy and fulfilled?" Whatever it is, find out and go for it. Where will you go, what will you do, no matter what the costs? When you discover what that is, tell yourself over and over again, "I am so excited that I get to do this. I'm going to do this because I *want* to, not because I have to."

Pick an amazing dream and go for it. Don't merely make a living; make a life. Launch out farther than you've ever gone before. Today, you have a shot at forever. Somebody is going to do something big, so ask yourself, "Why not me?" Why not take a chance?

Many people have a fire burning within them, something they feel compelled to do, or an idea or a project they strongly feel they should develop. Yet too often, they push those dreams into a subconscious drawer and never really give them a chance to be fulfilled. Frequently, the reason we allow our dreams and desires to be tamped into a dark black hole is because somebody rejected us or said no to us.

But one of the keys to learning how to write your epitaph while you're living is to look for opportunities, rather than obstacles, regardless of what other people say or do.

I've never had much appreciation for the word "no." Instead, I prefer "perseverance" or "persistence." Much more than talent or a pleasant personality, perseverance and persistence will open doors for you, if you simply keep working toward your goal and refuse to give up.

Although I am one of the best known astronauts in American history, believe it or not, I was not accepted the first time I applied to become a NASA astronaut, as I already mentioned.

At that time, NASA wanted test pilots, not scientists. I was a fighter pilot and an egghead, a scientist studying at MIT. Before leaving Germany, where I was flying practice bombing runs, I read that to become an astronaut, one had to train as a test pilot. Because I had chosen not to do that, I assumed there was little chance of me getting into the space program.

Nevertheless, I was convinced that I could be selected as an astronaut. Ed White had been accepted, and we had flown together in the Air Force during the cold war between the Soviet Union and the United States. I knew Ed was a good fighter pilot, and I was, too. "I can shoot gunnery as well as if not better than Ed can," I said. "I'm going to apply to be an astronaut."

But I was rejected. That could have been an insurmountable obstacle for me, or a barrier that detoured my entire life. But I was persistent. Sure, I was disappointed, but I didn't give up.

I learned more about NASA's Gemini program and talked with Gus Grissom, who was going to fly in that program; I also talked with the designer of the Gemini spacecraft.

I got into great physical shape, went to Houston, and applied again in 1963. This time I was accepted, along with a couple of other fighter pilots who, like me, had not been test pilots.

When the orders came out, I was again disappointed to discover that I was assigned to a backup crew, not a flight crew. I was not scheduled to fly during the entire Gemini program. Then one of those events over which I had no control but that would change the course of my life took place on February 28, 1966. While flying a routine flight from Houston to St. Louis, aboard a T-38 Talon, two of my astronaut friends, Charlie Bassett—my backdoor neighbor—and Elliot See, were killed when their plane missed the runway in foggy weather and crashed.

Their tragic deaths pushed Jim Lovell and me ahead on the list of astronauts, first as the backup crew for Gemini 9, and then as a flight crew, ready to fly on Gemini 12. Although I had nothing to do with it, and was deeply distraught over the deaths of my friends, had it not been for the freak accident, I would not have flown during the Gemini program. But because I went into space on Gemini 12, and even did a long space walk, those events set me in line for Apollo, and an eventual landing on the Moon.

That's one of the reasons why I have always tried to remind people that I was simply a guy who was in the right place at the right time. Yes, I had a great, supportive family, a strong work ethic, and wonderful friends. Yes, I studied incessantly, worked hard, and prepared in my areas of expertise, but perhaps the key to any success in life is to be ready when the opportunity comes along.

Sometimes if you think too long about something you want to do or some risk you want to take, you talk yourself out of it. On the other hand, if you muster your courage and just boldly step out and do it, you find that doors open for you that other people say are impossible to go through.

In 2010, President Barack Obama planned to speak at the Kennedy Space Center and make some announcements about the space program. I was in Washington, D.C., at the time, so I called Christina in California and said, "I want to get on Air Force One." I knew that because of post-9/11 security precautions, it was quite difficult to hitch a ride with the president, even for an astronaut, but I had confidence that it would work out.

Actually, I had flown aboard Air Force One previously when Neil, Mike, and I traveled around the world on behalf of President Richard Nixon on the goodwill tour following our landing on the Moon. Because the president was not along with us, the White House referred to the plane as Air Force *Two,* rather than Air Force One, but it was definitely the president's plane.

On another occasion, when I was at the Reagan Presidential Library in California for a book signing, Christina and I crashed a tour of his retired Air Force One. The tour guide didn't notice us at first, but when I asked a question, the guide recognized me. After all the other folks left, the tour guide gave us a personal tour, allowing me to compare the Reagan plane with the Nixon edition that I knew.

So as much as I understood that it would take some special circumstances to fall into place for me to get on President Obama's version of Air Force One, I refused to give up.

Christina continued checking every option, and I went from one government official to another, asking for permission to accompany the president. Our friends in the White House said, "Tell Buzz to get himself to Florida, and we'll have special VIP access for him once he arrives at Kennedy Space Center." I appreciated that, but that wasn't what I wanted. I wanted to fly on Air Force One so I could have a chance to talk with the president about my Mars Cycler. We were going to the same place, after all. What was so hard about giving me a ride? Of course, I was aware of security concerns, but I wouldn't take no for an answer, so I just kept talking to people who might be able to help.

Everyone in the White House told Christina and me, "You're not getting on Air Force One." But we continued to pursue every contact we had.

Finally, Christina received an email from her White House contact, saying, "Tell Buzz to meet the shuttle to Air Force One at the West Wing of the White House." Peter Marquez, former White House director of space policy, was able to join me. We were transported from the White House to Andrews

Air Force Base, and the official car drove us right to the enormous jet's staircase.

A short time later, I called Christina—from the president's jet—and said, "Hi, Christina, I'm on Air Force One."

The plane itself was very comfortable, with huge seats, as well as desks and chairs for working. The conference room aboard the aircraft is replete with video screens and teleconferencing capabilities. And, of course, there is free Wi-Fi aboard Air Force One!

The aircraft was impressive, but I was most taken with the gracious staff, all of whom had favorite Air Force One stories and were more than willing to share them if Peter and I would listen. We listened to a few, but I was too busy making phone calls to all my friends to focus on the attendants' stories, especially since the flight from Andrews to the Kennedy Space Center was relatively short.

After a while, I said to Peter, "Do you want to go look around?"

"Sure thing," Peter replied.

We started roaming around the president's plane and made it all the way to the stairs that led to the upper section of the Boeing 747 when an attendant spotted us. At first I thought he was going to reprimand us for exploring or send us back to our seats, but instead, he asked, "Would you like to see the cockpit?"

I smiled like I'd just won the lottery. "Of course," I replied. There were no security worries aboard Air Force One, so the attendant took us to the cockpit and I stuck my head inside the doorway. Not only had we made it onto Air Force One when all the naysayers said it was impossible, but I was now looking over the shoulders of the guys who were flying it.

Unlike flying commercially, it was not necessary to turn off my phone before landing. In fact, nobody even came on the intercom instructing us to sit down and buckle up. The pilots of the huge plane brought it down smooth as a feather right on the space shuttle runway at the Kennedy Space Center and then eased to a stop.

When we arrived, President Obama and I walked out to greet the crowd to whom he was going to speak. Even though we had very limited time together, I didn't want to miss an opportunity to tell the president about my research and the Aldrin Mars Cycler, the method I had developed for going to Mars. As we were walking, I quickly explained my plans for the Cycler concept. I told the president that we needed to use Phobos, one of the two moons of Mars, as our staging point before we actually landed on Mars. He was planning to promise an increase in NASA's funding by six billion dollars, and to orbit Mars within the next two decades. I was talking about *landing* on Mars.

The daughter of a friend of mine had made a papier-mâché model of Phobos that was so good I carried it with me wherever I traveled, so I could illustrate how the Mars Cycler works. As I was talking with President Obama, I remembered that I had the model in my briefcase. I pulled out the papier-mâché model, which looked similar to a large baked potato, and was using it to explain my concepts to the president.

The president took the model from my hands and began to walk away with it. "Well, thank you, Buzz," he said, waving.

"No, no, no! That's my Phobos!" I said. The president must have thought I intended him to have the model. I didn't.

I had taken that model on so many trips and had shown it to so many people, my papier-mâché Phobos was beginning to fray and show cracks, so much so that the aluminum foil beneath the papier-mâché had begun to show. A few weeks later, we were having a "full moon" party at my home. As a joke, Christina placed the Phobos model in the middle of a table in my office and wrote out a warning: "Moon rock. Please don't touch!"

Throughout the party, guests slipped into my office to view my many mementos, and there was the Phobos model. "Ohh, look, it's a Moon rock!" a number of people gushed.

Really? I actually do have some Moon rocks but none of them are made from papier-mâché! And I don't leave them sitting on my desk.

I had made a presentation in 2009 for the Augustine Commission, a committee of experts assigned with the task of reviewing the U.S. human spaceflight plans regarding recommendations for the future of the space program. In an effort to encourage further exploration and to avoid duplication of our efforts, I made the comment, "Why go back to the Moon again? Been there and done that." I was saying it facetiously.

In 2010, President Obama picked up on parts of my presentation and repeated some of my recommendations practically verbatim in his speech at the Kennedy Space Center. But not in the way that I intended.

"Why do we need to go back to the Moon?" the president asked. "As Buzz says, 'Been there, done that.'"

I learned a lesson through that experience. Be careful what you say, nowadays, because it might be repeated—maybe even by the president of the United States!

(

JUST BECAUSE I AM PASSIONATE ABOUT motivating people to explore Mars doesn't mean that I think we should forget about developing projects on the Moon. I know we can enjoy numerous benefits by exploring and building an outpost of some sort on the Moon. My friend Stephen Hawking, the English physicist, feels the same way. Stephen had invited me to visit on several occasions, but it simply never worked out. Then on March 14, 2015, Albert Einstein's birthday, I was speaking at Oxford and Cambridge universities in Great Britain, and some friends offered to take Christina, my family, and me to Hawking's home in Cambridge, where we were able to spend an afternoon together. Stephen has stated publicly, "We have made remarkable progress in the last hundred years, but if we want to continue, our future is in space." I am in complete agreement with him, so I was excited to learn more of his thoughts.

Stephen suffers from amyotrophic lateral sclerosis (ALS), is wheelchair bound, and is unable to talk without the use of a specially adapted computer hooked to a speech-generating device that simulates a voice. It is difficult to have a conversation with him, however, because he has to answer by using the computer and it takes him a long time to reply. When we visited, I gave him a long monologue about my plans for the Mars Cycler. Stephen listened intently. After a while, I asked Stephen, "Well, what do you think?"

We waited a long time for Stephen's response. Finally, he managed to say, "Why not the Moon first?"

I smiled and promised to send Stephen my book *Mission to Mars* and a digital version of my entire discourse on how we can successfully colonize Mars. Although I don't want to ignore the Moon, I do want the next generation to go where no humans have previously traveled. There are entire vistas yet to be explored.

Granted, there are times when you have to change directions or try another method to achieve your goals. It takes courage to say something isn't working, so let's try something different. For instance, President Obama took a lot of heat when he canceled the Constellation program—a human spaceflight mission begun by NASA in 2005 but discontinued in 2010—but that was part of my recommendation. The program wasn't working, and it never would work, so why keep pouring money into it? To me, it was not about politics. I am all in favor of support for space exploration, regardless of party affiliation. The president inherited a bad program when he came into office. Constellation had been regarded as the next big thing in space, but it wasn't working, and NASA knew it and so did everybody else.

The problem was exacerbated, however, because President George W. Bush had already established the time line for the completion of the space shuttle program, after which the shuttles would be retired and used mainly as museum pieces. I encouraged both President Bush and President Obama to extend the shuttle program, which we could easily do by further stretching out the time between flights, and that would extend the program a little longer. Without the shuttle program, we had no readily available ability to get to the International Space Station (ISS)—which we had built but could no longer reach without reliance upon the Russians or the Chinese. When we completed the shuttle missions, we already had a deal in place with the Russians to transport our astronauts to the ISS, but at the whopping price of $55 million per American astronaut! As soon as the shuttle program ended, the Russians upped the price to $75 million per astronaut—quite a capitalistic move.

After the Constellation program was canceled, NASA toyed with another quirky idea, the Space Launch System (SLS) program, derisively called the "Senate Launch System" by critics, among whom I could be counted. I was asked to take part in a U.S. Senate subcommittee meeting in Washington, D.C., to present my thoughts about the program.

At one point during my comments, I didn't use much tact. "Can you believe that they are using Heritage components to build the SLS?" I groused. "Do you know what that means? It's old stuff. That's not what America is all about!"

One of the staffers spoke up. "In full disclosure, sir, I'm the one who wrote that law."

Oops! It was the old foot-in-mouth syndrome. I tried to say something positive, but the only thing that came out of my mouth was, "Well, it's stupid!"

So much for my space ambassadorship!

But it *was* stupid to use old parts in a new space program. We need to be forward thinking!

The world was quite impressed in July 2015, when the New Horizons spacecraft flew past the planet Pluto, after being launched on January 19, 2006, on its journey venturing deeper into the mysterious Kuiper belt and beyond. Now that takes patience and perseverance. It was nearly ten years before New Horizons sent fascinating photographs of Pluto back to Earth. I was happy for the progress, but I was even more impressed when the European Space Agency's Rosetta team caught up to and landed an unmanned satellite on a comet on November 12, 2014, and started sending photos back to Earth. Do you have any idea how difficult that was? Wow, talk about the ultimate rendezvous experience! I had been hoping that we could land on an asteroid, a much larger mountain of rock hurtling through space, but the Rosetta team did even better— landing on a speeding comet! The comet was much farther away from Earth than Mars ever is. Moreover, to control a landing on a moving, rotating comet, with communications transmissions limited to the speed of light, is incredibly impressive! That's the kind of "never give up" spirit that I hope we can foster in the next group of U.S. space pioneers.

(

OF COURSE, I WELCOME EVERY OPPORTUNITY to keep space exploration in the news. For some reason, though, the Obama

Administration had decided to ignore the 45th anniversary of the Apollo 11 landing in 2014. Christina and I bugged everyone we knew who had any political clout, saying, "Every U.S. president has met with the Apollo 11 astronauts to commemorate the anniversary of the initial Moon landing every five years. Surely you don't want to be known as the first administration to eliminate that tradition. This is not merely American history; this is world history."

Finally, the Obama White House conceded and agreed to have the president briefly meet with the Apollo 11 astronauts on the 45th anniversary of the first Moon landing. They refused, however, to allow our family members to attend the meeting, another departure from tradition. With every previous administration, regardless of political persuasion, the family members of Apollo 11 were always welcomed.

Christina, however, had learned an important lesson from the Air Force One incident. She refused to take no for an answer. She called another friend in the White House and requested that the family members be permitted to attend the meeting with the president.

"They are not going to let the family members in," Christina's White House contact reiterated. Nevertheless, Christina remained undaunted.

She called my family members and said, "You get on the vehicle transporting Carol Armstrong (Neil's widow), Mike, and Buzz."

She then called me and said, "When you are meeting with the president, casually mention that your family is outside in the White House reception area."

When I greeted the president, I told him that my daughter, Jan, my grandson, Jeffry, and my son Andy were outside waiting on me. Sure enough, the president responded, "Oh, well, bring them inside."

I smiled and said, "Why, thank you, Mr. President."

Because of that persistence, Mike Collins's daughter, Kate, was able to meet the president as well.

Sometimes you just have to be persistent, and you cannot take no for an answer. Don't listen to the naysayers, the people who give you all the reasons why something cannot be done or tell you it's never been done that way before. I love it when someone tells me something cannot be done, or that nobody has ever done it before. What a challenge! What an opportunity to go where nobody else has ever gone. When you are told no, do not stop and do not give up. Try again and find a new way.

What idea have you stuffed inside your drawer? What could you do to give birth or rebirth to that idea? Today is the day to get started. Don't allow anything to deter you. You may not know everything you need to know, but you know enough to get started. Don't wait for someone to write complimentary things about you after you are dead and gone. Do your epitaph while you are living!

Nothing is impossible, but you must have a passion for what you want to do and a plan for where you want to go if you ever hope to get there. It was "impossible" when President John F. Kennedy announced in 1961 that the United States was going to land on the Moon before the end of that decade. At the time, we had barely gotten our space program off the ground. But we did it. Nothing is impossible if you believe.

The "impossible" just takes a little longer.

Develop that inner perseverance, that attitude that says, I can do this; I will do this! No matter what the opposition says, I will find a way.

Remember: Can't never could. No never will. Success comes in "cans."

# CHAPTER SIX

# MAINTAIN YOUR SPIRIT
# OF ADVENTURE.

You don't have to go to the Moon to maintain a sense of wonder in life. You just need to foster an adventurous spirit. I find tremendous pleasure in the "little things," everywhere I go.

For instance, I prefer to sit by the window in an airplane so I can look out at the marvelous sights. To this day, I am still thrilled when I fly into New York City, and the plane circles around the Statue of Liberty before coming in for a landing. Powerful emotions well within me as I look out the plane's window at Lady Liberty, and feelings of pride and patriotism surge through me.

I enjoy flying across the United States. In my mid-80s, after orbiting the Earth in Gemini 12 and walking on the Moon during Apollo 11, I'm still amazed as I gaze out a plane window, observing the clouds and the astounding terrain of Earth below as we fly. *How many years did it take for the Colorado River to carve out the Grand Canyon?* I ponder as I fly over Arizona. *What cataclysmic events took place that heaved the majestic Rocky Mountains into place?* I'm a scientist and an astronaut, but looking down at creation from an altitude of 37,000 feet, as I zoom across the country in a metal tube, I have to wonder, *How did it all happen? It couldn't have been simply a cosmic accident.*

I'm even more fascinated with watching Christina and her husband Alex's baby Logan developing. I missed those years with my own kids because I was so consumed with work. But now, I observe with awe how little baby Logan responds to various stimuli, amazed at how the neurotransmitters in his young brain are snapping to attention and discovering the world around him. Each day is a new adventure for him, as he looks at life with awe. I hope to always maintain that same sort of childlike fascination with life here on Earth as well as on other celestial bodies.

Although I've had some unique experiences in space, I still have an adventurous spirit here on Earth. I've traveled "up" to the North Pole on a Russian nuclear-powered icebreaker ship with former television newscaster Hugh Downs and his wife, Ruth. Hugh had a film crew for the ABC television program *20/20* documenting our trip.

It was freezing cold when we reached the North Pole, but in my mind, I could almost hear Karen Carpenter, one of my all-time favorite female artists, singing, "I'm on top of the world looking down on creation." We shuttled across the frozen expanse by helicopter to a location where we were served a meal on the ice. Then some of the passengers set up a makeshift baseball diamond on the ice and we played softball at the North Pole. What an experience! A couple of the younger passengers even found a spot where the ice had cleared and they dared to jump in the water for a quick swim—very quick! But not me. I'm adventurous, but I'm not crazy!

I've traveled 250,000 miles *up* to the Moon, and *up* to the North Pole, and I've also plunged *down* more than 2.4 miles, all the way to the ocean floor in a tiny, yellow, French submersible to view the wreckage of the *Titanic*. The company that sponsored the trip hoped to raise a section of the ship's hull and conduct an unprecedented exploration of the bow. Unlike the Beatles' hypothetical yellow submarine, the submersible was spherical in shape, with thick, strong glass portholes on each side that allowed the two French operators and me to look out.

This was not a luxury liner like the *Titanic*. Quite the contrary, the sub was a claustrophobic person's worst nightmare, with the pilot sitting so he could work the control board as the copilot and I lay flat on our stomachs on the floor. There was no restroom aboard.

The operators spoke only a bit of broken English, so communication was difficult. I had taken French in high school, and with a lot of pointing at the menu, I might have been able to order something to eat in a Parisian restaurant, but that was the extent of my foreign language knowledge.

I did my best to understand the Frenchmens' instructions and conversations.

It took an hour and a half for us to descend through the lonely darkness, until we finally caught sight of the sunken ship, eerily resting on the ocean floor. It was total blackness all around, the only illumination cast from the submersible's lights. I grabbed a camera and started shooting pictures of the ship, festooned with rusting metal that looked like gingerbread, as I imagined passengers once standing on the bow, looking over the railing made famous by James Cameron's movie, now covered with a surreal white algae and other organisms.

The French operators worked for nearly nine hours attempting to strategically place lift bags that they hoped would cause a portion of the *Titanic*'s hull to float. But as the pilot attempted to raise the hull, a cable snapped, and another would not release, dooming the mission. The *Titanic* yawned in resistance and settled back to sleep, as though it knew our efforts had been scrubbed as a failure. But it was not a failure for me. I had traveled to the ocean floor, to one of the sea's most guarded secrets.

(

IN 2010, AT 80 YEARS OF AGE, I hitched a ride on a gigantic whale shark while scuba diving in the Galápagos Islands.

I've never really had a hobby, but when I am not working, scuba diving is one of my favorite things to do, and under the sea is my favorite place to be—on *this* planet. To this day, I enjoy scuba diving excursions at least four or five times each year, to various locations around the world.

Besides the gorgeous sights waiting to be discovered, I love the quietness and the solitude of being under the sea. It is a part of life that cannot be described by mere words and can only be truly experienced by going underwater. No cell phones are ringing; I have no emails to answer, although with wristwatches now boasting more computer power than Neil and I had in the lunar module when we landed on the Moon, I can see being online underwater as a possibility. For now, though, I love the natural peace that I find deep below the surface. To me, scuba diving is both relaxing and energizing at the same time—relaxing because it is so peaceful; energizing because the unparalleled sights inexorably call for exploration.

To help celebrate my 80th birthday, my son Andy took me on a special trip to the Galápagos Islands, located in the Pacific Ocean about 600 miles west of Ecuador. The waters off the Galápagos Islands, two uninhabitable islands known as Darwin and Wolf, feature some of the most picturesque and fascinating scuba diving opportunities in the world. It is also some of the most challenging diving in the world. The strong, cold currents do not make for easy diving, nor do the large numbers of dangerous sharks, but the waters around the islands are teeming with spectacular sea life. They are home to some of the largest whale sharks on the planet, some as large as 40 feet long, 18 feet high, and weighing in at more than 20 tons. To put that in perspective, imagine swimming up to a fish as large as a Greyhound bus.

Although whale sharks are enormous, they are relatively docile. They don't normally attack humans, because their favorite food is plankton. A whale shark has a flat-looking head and blunt snout, with massive, oval-shaped jaws that the fish opens frequently as it moves rapidly through the water, filtering everything in its path, discarding anything that isn't plankton.

Even though there is little danger of getting eaten by a whale shark, they are still dangerous to humans because their sleek bodies move so rapidly through the water, and a human is so small comparatively that the fish might smash right into a diver without missing a stroke or even noticing. If you get in the whale shark's way, you could get hurt, because the fish would flick you off like a gnat.

The whale sharks are so huge, they can be spotted from the air by a small plane or a helicopter pilot scouting the seas, who then radios the information to a boat captain, who points the craft in that direction.

Prior to entering the water, Ricardo, our indigenous dive master, cautioned us, "Do not touch the sea life, especially the whale sharks."

Andy gave me a look, as if to say, "And that means you, Dad." Of course, he knew that if I came anywhere near a whale shark, all bets were off, because I'd want to get as close as possible.

We paddled away from the boat in small Pangas, life rafts a lot like the more common inflatable rubber Zodiacs. Andy carried the underwater camera as he and Ricardo and I plunged into the water. The moment my body was submerged, I was in an entirely new world. The sunshine filtered through the turquoise blue Pacific waters above me, providing plenty of light by which to see. Almost immediately, I spotted a sharp-toothed moray eel easing out of a coral cave below me. I noticed a few small sharks and some large turtles, as well as a spectacular array of brightly colored tropical fish.

We had been underwater for a while, and I was about 75 feet below the surface when I saw a whale shark heading in our direction at an angle, and even from a distance, I could tell that the fish was enormous! Remember Jonah and the whale? This guy's mouth could have swallowed Jonah and a whole lot more!

I swam right at him, looking him in the eye the whole time. His huge mouth was closed, but I was still careful not to get in his way.

The whale shark was moving fast, so I didn't have much time to figure out my rendezvous plans, but with a bit of experience in that area, I quickly calculated the direction I needed to swim if I hoped to intersect with the fish. The dive master saw me and began waving frantically, trying to keep me from approaching the whale shark, but I started swimming on a trajectory in which I felt sure I could catch the huge creature's dorsal fin. Andy saw me, too, and must have instinctively figured out what I planned to do, because he swam as fast as he could with the camera ready.

I intercepted the whale shark, looked the fish in the eye, and then drifted back and above him, to where I knew the whale shark's dorsal fin would be coming by me in a moment. Sure enough, the whale shark passed below me, so I swam hard toward him, grabbed onto the dorsal fin, and held on for dear life! The whale shark didn't pay much attention to me. Quite the contrary, he didn't slow down a bit, swiftly carrying me along with him through the sea.

I could hear Ricardo sounding his alarm rattle, warning me away from the whale shark. I knew Ricardo would not be happy with me, but I continued to hang on. Worse yet, I knew my air supply was running low. I checked my air gauge as the whale shark continued swimming, with Ricardo and Andy chasing us from behind, Ricardo frantically urging me to let go and Andy hurrying to get as many photos as he could. By the time I let go of the whale shark's fin, I was almost completely out of air. I had to "buddy breathe" with Ricardo, taking a gulp of his air, and holding my breath as long as I could before taking another, sharing his air tank to get back to the surface. Ricardo was furious, though wonderfully gracious, especially considering that I had totally disobeyed his instructions. But how often does an 80-year-old man get to celebrate his birthday by hitching a ride on a whale shark?

Andy got some fantastic photos of me riding the whale shark, and I'm almost as proud of those shots as I am of the ones Neil Armstrong took of me on the Moon. When I met Brad Norman, an Australian scientist who is one of the world's foremost experts on whale sharks, I was reluctant to show him one of my pictures because I thought he might be upset at me for getting so close to the huge endangered fish.

Brad loved the photo! "We don't encourage the public to get near a whale shark, but I do it all the time, Buzz," he said,

*My handsome family. Top, left to right: A young man
named Buzz; my mother, Marion; my father, Edwin, Sr.
Bottom: My sisters, Maddy and Fay Ann.*

*We have spent summers at the New Jersey shore
my whole life. I still go there to see my extended family to this day.
This photo was probably taken in 1934.*

*Strong women helped shape me, especially my mother
(in the middle) and my two sisters, Maddy and Fay Ann.*
OPPOSITE: *I've always been curious about how things work.
Even as a young boy—here I am at six years old—I loved
to explore and was always looking for a new adventure.*

DEDICATION

    In the hopes that this work may in some way contribute to their exploration of space, this is dedicated to the crew members of this country's present and future manned space programs.  If only I could join them in their exciting endeavors!

TOP: *I was only 17 years old when I was accepted into the United States Military Academy at West Point. Here I am, a young plebe, proudly wearing my uniform.*
BOTTOM: *In the dedication of my MIT doctoral thesis, written in 1963, I expressed a hope that my work could help in the future of the space program. My dreams were more than realized.*

*In November 1966, Jim Lovell and I flew Gemini 12, the last of the Gemini missions. We orbited Earth for four days, during which I completed three tethered space walks, the first of their kind.*

*I snapped this photo of myself during one*
*of my Gemini 12 space walks. Little did I know,*
*I was pioneering the art of the selfie in 1966!*
OPPOSITE: *Neil Armstrong took this iconic photo*
*of me on the Moon during our Apollo 11 mission*
*in July 1969. I think he was a pretty good photographer,*
*as this picture was quite spontaneous.*

TOP: *I took very few photos on the Moon, because Neil*
*had the camera while I set up the experiments.*
*My son Andy finds it ironic: I never take photos,*
*but one of the few I took has become a historic one!*
BOTTOM: *My bootprint on the Moon looked lonely,*
*so I took another one with my boot in the frame.*

# TRAVEL VOUCHER
## MEMORANDUM

| | |
|---|---|
| DEPARTMENT, BUREAU, OR ESTABLISHMENT<br>NASA - Manned Spacecraft Center | VOUCHER NO. 014501 |
| PAYEE'S NAME<br>Col. Edwin E. Aldrin 00018 | SCHEDULE NO. |
| MAILING ADDRESS **PLEASE MAKE CHECK PAYABLE TO:**<br>Nassau Bay National Bank<br>P.O. Box 58008<br>Houston, Texas 77032   Account #1-0348-9 | PAID BY |

| OFFICIAL DUTY STATION<br>Houston, Texas | RESIDENCE | | |
|---|---|---|---|

| FOR TRAVEL AND OTHER EXPENSES | | TRAVEL ADVANCE | | CHECK NO. |
|---|---|---|---|---|
| FROM (DATE)<br>7-7-69 | TO (DATE)<br>7-27-69 | Outstanding | $ | |
| APPLICABLE TRAVEL AUTHORIZATION(S) | | Amount to be applied | | CASH PAYMENT OF $_____<br>RECEIVED (DATE)_____ |
| NO.<br>X-22002 | DATE<br>6/18/69 | Balance to remain<br>outstanding | $ | |

## TRANSPORTATION REQUESTS ISSUED

| TRANSPORTATION REQUEST NUMBER | AGENT'S VALUATION OF TICKET | INITIALS OF CARRIER ISSUING TICKET | MODE, CLASS OF SERVICE, AND ACCOMMODATIONS * | DATE ISSUED | POINTS OF TRAVEL | |
|---|---|---|---|---|---|---|
| | | | | | FROM— | TO— |
| Gov. Air | | | | | Houston, Texas | Cape Kennedy, Fla.<br>Moon<br>Pacific Ocean<br>(USN Hornett)<br>Hawaii<br>and return to Houston, Texas |

| | Dollars | Cts |
|---|---|---|
| 8-4-69   AMOUNT CLAIMED → | 33 | 31 |

| APPROVED (Supervisory and other approvals when required) | DIFFERENCES: | | |
|---|---|---|---|

| NEXT PREVIOUS VOUCHER PAID UNDER SAME TRAVEL AUTHORITY | | | Total verified correct for charge to appropriation(s)<br>(initials) | 33 | 31 |
|---|---|---|---|---|---|
| VOUCHER NO. | D.O. SYMBOL | DATE (MONTH-YEAR) | Applied to travel advance (appropriation symbol) | | |

AUG 2 6 1969 ———— C. W. Bird
Authorized Certifying Officer

| NET TO TRAVELER → | 33 | 31 |
|---|---|---|

ACCOUNTING CLASSIFICATION
039-00-00-00-CA-2031-CB11

*My travel voucher to the Moon and back;*
*I was reimbursed $33.31 for a rental car to get*
*to the Kennedy Space Center in time for the launch.*

*Scuba diving is my favorite thing to do on* this *planet.*

*My son Andy took this photo of me hitching a ride on a whale shark in June 2010 during a dive we did near the Galápagos Islands to celebrate my 80th birthday.*

*My Mission Control Director, Christina Korp, keeps me in line,
but we also have a lot of fun together. Here we are
at Nova Spacefest in Tucson, Arizona, on April 1, 2012.*

LEFT: *I love how curious kids are. Whenever my Mascot #1,
Brielle Korp, wants to know how something works, I'm happy to show her.*
RIGHT: *I have always wanted to go faster and higher, so of course
I went (with Christina and my Mascot #2, Logan Korp)
to visit the Burj Khalifa in Dubai—the tallest building
in the world, with more than 160 stories.*

*As soon as I got this T-shirt from Christina, I knew
it was my new call sign: Get Your Ass to Mars!*

*I have always admired Stephen Hawking, and I am proud
that we have become friends. Here I visited him at his home
in Cambridge, United Kingdom, in March 2015.*

TOP: *I showed my model of Phobos, one of the Mars moons, to President Obama at the Kennedy Space Center in 2010, and he thought I was trying to give it to him. He almost walked away with it!*
BOTTOM: *I gave testimony to Senator Ted Cruz during a Senate hearing on commercializing space in March 2015. I try to bug Congress to invest in space as much as possible in between my busy travels.*

*Lady Liberty is always a welcome sight whenever
I get to New York City—especially by helicopter.*
OPPOSITE: *I enjoyed my part on* The Simpsons, *but
I'm especially proud that I made it as one of the show's
top 25 guest stars; and I got my own figurine!*

*At Stonehenge in March 2015 I decided
to send a message to the cosmos.*

"because I have to tag them." Brad uses NASA star-tracking technology to track the whale sharks around the world, and to study their movements. I was especially honored when Brad named a whale shark "Apollo" in my honor. I have enjoyed making the world more aware of this beautiful fish. When I tell this story in schools, I'm careful to include the caution, "Kids, don't try this at home!"

(

ALWAYS KEEP SOME NEW, exciting adventure on your "bucket list," that list of things you want to do before you die. Maybe you'll want to swim with the sharks, too. One thing I still want to do is to go to the South Pole. I've been to the North Pole, but never to Antarctica. Another experience I still want to have is an underwater diving adventure with some crocodiles.

Really!

My son Andy has embraced my penchant for exploration and adventure. He is brilliant, much smarter than I am, and has a PhD from UCLA. He wrote the foreword to my book *Mission to Mars*. As a father, I could not possibly be more proud of him. In recent years, Andy has become more involved in trying to help bring my scientific concepts to fruition. It means a great deal to me that Andy has chosen to carry on my work. Although I am proud of all my children, Andy is more similar to me, in that he is always up for almost anything I'm willing to try.

For instance, not long ago, Andy found a place in Africa where we could do a diving expedition with crocodiles. We seriously considered doing it, but after thinking through the risks, we decided to put that trip on hold.

I still have an adventurous spirit, but at my age, sometimes I also have to be sensible. After all, crocodiles are pretty fast, and I wondered if I could outrun a croc on land. I felt confident that I could probably outswim a crocodile in my scuba gear underwater, but if it caught up to me and I had to make a hasty exit on land, wearing flippers on my feet, a wet suit, and a heavy air tank on my back, I'm not so sure I could outdistance it. I decided I didn't want to lose a hand! As a result, Andy and I chose to forgo that trip—for now—but we haven't given up on it.

*Really!*

You don't have to do some of the more outlandish things that I do to enjoy an adventurous spirit, but you do need to stay active. Ideally, you should find some activity that you can do year-round. Staying active and maintaining a sense of adventure are important for anyone, but are especially essential as we get a little older.

People often ask me how I stay in such good physical shape. "I walk fast through airports," I tell them. When it comes to exercise, I subscribe to the Neil Armstrong philosophy. At least half seriously, Neil always said, "God only gave me so many heartbeats; I'm not going to waste any of them on physical exercise!"

Truth is, I keep moving and I stay active, and until I take my last breath, I want to maintain my fascination with life and my sense of adventure. With that attitude, I might just live forever!

# CHAPTER SEVEN

# FAILURE IS ALWAYS AN OPTION.

**P**eople who say "Failure is not an option" are usually trying to motivate others to excellence, and that is noble. But the truth is, if you are afraid to fail, you will probably not accomplish much in life. Imagine if failure were not an option for the space program. We'd have never gotten off the ground.

Years after I had walked on the Moon, my son Andy examined the launch records of the Atlas rocket system, used in four Mercury launches, including Friendship 7, the spacecraft in which John Glenn became the first U.S. astronaut to orbit Earth three times. When Andy studied the history of the Atlas rockets, the precursor to the Saturn rockets used for the Apollo program, he was shocked to discover that they had experienced a 40 percent failure rate.

Andy quips that our first astronauts may have had enormous courage, but their sense of judgment must have been seriously impaired! For Apollo 11, we had estimated a 60 percent chance of landing successfully on the Moon and a 95 percent chance of returning home safely. I especially liked that last part!

President Richard Nixon possessed great confidence in the mission of Apollo 11, but he was also a realist. He knew it was possible for us to fail in our attempt to land on the Moon and return home. In a little known document, the president prepared a "what if?" speech in case Neil and I didn't make it. His words are honoring though sobering:

> Fate has ordained that the men who went to the moon to explore in peace will stay on the moon to rest in peace.
>
> These brave men, Neil Armstrong and Edwin Aldrin, know that there is no hope for their recovery. But they also know that there is hope for mankind in their sacrifice.
>
> These two men are laying down their lives in mankind's most noble goal: the search for truth and understanding.
>
> They will be mourned by their families and friends; they will be mourned by their nation; they will be mourned by the people of the world; they will be mourned by a Mother Earth that dared send two of her sons into the unknown.

In their exploration, they stirred the people of the world to feel as one; in their sacrifice, they bind more tightly the brotherhood of man.

In ancient days, men looked at stars and saw their heroes in the constellations. In modern times, we do much the same, but our heroes are epic men of flesh and blood.

Others will follow, and surely find their way home. Man's search will not be denied. But these men were the first, and they will remain the foremost in our hearts.

For every human being who looks up at the moon in the nights to come will know that there is some corner of another world that is forever mankind.

The president was wise to consider the possibilities and would have been remiss had he not. All these years later, when I read President Nixon's prepared but undelivered speech, written for him by presidential speechwriter and noted journalist William Safire, it reminds me that failure is always an option.

( 

IF YOU WANT TO DO SOMETHING SIGNIFICANT, something noble, something that perhaps has never been done before, you must be willing to fail. And don't be surprised or devastated when you do. It is not the end of the world, and untold numbers of people have experienced major failures and have come back from them, not only as more successful, but also as better, stronger people.

I failed miserably during one of my first experiments on the Moon. With Neil already on the lunar surface, I made my way out of the *Eagle*'s hatch and began carefully descending the ladder, stepping slowly until I became more accustomed to how the heavy life-support backpack was going to affect my sense of balance in an environment with only one-sixth the gravitational pull of Earth's. When I reached the last rung on the ladder, I jumped down to the *Eagle*'s footpad, solidly planted on the surface.

According to our flight plan's checklist, I was supposed to jump back up again to the bottom rung, as an experiment from which I could learn how much energy I needed to expend after Neil and I returned from exploring the Moon's surface. Because it had never been done before, we wanted to make sure that we could comfortably negotiate that first step after our extra-vehicular activity.

Neil had easily made the jump from the lunar module's pad back to the first step, a leap I had watched him make as I peered out the window before going down the ladder myself. It didn't look too hard.

But when I tried to jump back to the first rung, I under-estimated the gravitational pull of the Moon, didn't jump high enough, and missed the step by about an inch. My shins skidded against the step and scraped the bottom of the rung, smearing Moon dust on my space suit just below my knees.

The dust was apparently a residual effect, left over from the bottom of Neil's boots on the ladder.

So my first experiment on the Moon was a failure. *How embarrassing!* I thought.

My botched jump shook my confidence a bit. Maybe moving around on the Moon would be more difficult than I'd anticipated. I stood on the LM's footpad for a few moments to regain my composure, and that's when I decided to test the urine-collection device.

*I'll put a little more oomph in it,* I thought to myself before jumping up again, and this time I easily ascended to the bottom rung. I was back to where I started a few seconds earlier but now with greatly improved self-confidence and a much lighter bladder. I dropped back down to the footpad and stepped out to where only one human being had ever gone before me, and that only a short time earlier—I stepped onto the surface of the Moon.

Over the years of my life, I've been quite open about the failures I've endured. I find that many people can relate more to my mistakes than they can to my successes. In truth, they both go hand in hand; my failures have led to my successes, and some of my greatest achievements have set me up for my worst falls. But I've learned and I've grown from both kinds of experiences.

Some people don't like to admit that they have failed or that they have not yet achieved their goals or lived up to their own expectations. But failure is not a sign of weakness. It is a sign that you are alive and growing.

Get out of your comfort zone and be willing to take some risks as you work on new tasks. Some individuals have an aversion to risks, but it is not foolish to accept a level of risk, as long as the magnitude and worthiness of the goal you are seeking to achieve is commensurate with your risk. As your comfort zone expands, seek out even greater challenges. It is often said, and it really is true: You can do almost anything if you put your mind to it.

(

KEEP IN MIND THAT progress is not always linear. It takes constant course correcting and often a lot of zigzagging. Unfortunate things happen, accidents occur, and setbacks are usually painful, but that does not mean we quit.

My two biggest regrets both involve matters that I wish I would have spoken up about more vociferously: a space walk and the space shuttle.

On Gemini 9, NASA had hoped to conduct an experiment using an untethered jet pack during a space walk. I really wanted to do that! Imagine floating around in space and navigating under your own power as you orbit the Earth at 17,000 miles an hour.

I'm not a big movie buff, although I enjoy movies when I have time to watch them. Of course, I enjoy science fiction and I especially love movies about space, even though some of the older movies get so many details wrong. But they were imaginative in their time, and helped inspire us to reach for the stars.

One of my early favorites was *2001: A Space Odyssey,* a movie adapted from a story written by sci-fi master Arthur C. Clarke that came out in 1968, when I was training for the Apollo program. I'm embarrassed to admit it, but I was really tired the evening I attended the premiere and I fell asleep during the movie, despite Stanley Kubrick's brilliant production and amazing special effects. But it is still one of my favorites!

More recently, I really enjoyed *Gravity,* starring Sandra Bullock and George Clooney. Although the movie had some errors (my friend Neil deGrasse Tyson enjoys pointing them out) and bent the laws of physics during the free-falling interaction between the characters, it came close to depicting the reality and awkwardness of moving around in zero gravity. As someone who has actually "walked" in space, I cringed while watching emergencies on the screen that I had hoped would never happen. But for the person who has never experienced space travel, the movie's portrayals are thrilling because it graphically shows the hazards and the dangers of space walks if things go wrong. When I came out of the movie theater, I said to myself and to others, "Sandra Bullock deserves an Oscar."

Unfortunately, during Gemini 12, NASA considered the risks too great for me to do the Clooney-type space walk. I had trained underwater to get comfortable with neutral buoyancy, so I felt confident that I could carry out the difficult procedures required to be able to "free-maneuver" with only a jet pack outside the spacecraft.

But NASA greatly wanted to avoid any failures on the final Gemini mission, so they canceled the experiment. I was extremely disappointed when I received the news, so I objected and tried to convince my superiors that we could accomplish the jet pack space walk. They listened, but were entrenched in their position. No jet pack for me.

I did the space walk during Gemini 12, but I didn't have a jet pack, and I remained tethered to the Gemini 12 spacecraft. Certainly, I was thrilled to have experienced the sensational space walk outside the capsule. Please don't misunderstand: I'm grateful for all my experiences in space, but I will always regret not speaking up more strongly, and possibly having the opportunity to operate detached from the spacecraft, using the jet pack. Because we didn't attempt to spacewalk with the jet pack, we lost valuable time in which the technology for maneuvering in space could have progressed much more rapidly. On the other hand, I knew that if NASA did not deem the experiment safe and something went wrong, I might still be floating around somewhere in space, so I resigned myself to being content. Later, during the space shuttle and space station missions, astronauts were able to maneuver on their own using the jet packs. Lucky dogs!

My second regret is much more serious. I regret that I didn't warn NASA more emphatically about the problems I saw with the space shuttle.

Shortly after I returned to Earth, after Apollo 11, I attended a meeting in Huntsville, Alabama, to view new spacecraft designs and to learn about a new space program along with a number of NASA officials, aerospace engineers, and rocket manufacturers. This program was intended to be NASA's next big step, after Apollo.

While there, I was somewhat surprised to learn that our next foray into space would include an orbiter with wings and with wheels that could land on a runway, as well as a booster, also with wings and wheels to land on a runway. The program had generated great interest. At the meeting, at least seven aerospace manufacturers touted their rockets and boosters on which they were already working. They had models built in 1970 regarding the seven configurations and stages of the program to follow Apollo.

Today, we would be delighted to have a fully reusable orbiter to take the crew only, a booster to get them there, and then a return to Earth for both of them. We'd love to have that.

Why don't we have that? Because of a grave design flaw.

When I studied the models, I observed that the boosters in the models had windows. That was a surprise to me. After all, why would you want windows in a booster with nobody in it?

I was informed that a crew of two astronauts would travel inside the booster to the space station, and then return in the booster to land back on Earth.

I worried about the crew in the booster during launch and said so. I thought it was unwise because of the expense, but even more so because of the danger to the astronauts.

During a launch, if something goes wrong, the top concern is for the safety of the astronauts in the orbiter. Generally, the lower stages of a launch can be destroyed relatively easily, simply by triggering the "Destruct" button. But that step could not be taken safely with a crew sitting atop the rocket in a booster.

I didn't make a big deal about it at the meeting in Huntsville, but I spoke candidly about my concerns when I returned to the Manned Space Center in Houston. I should have spoken more strongly and been more emphatic. Perhaps if I had objected in front of the aerospace companies that had done the studies about manned boosters versus unmanned boosters, I could have made a case for the safety of the astronauts.

The NASA people who would be sitting in the control center during ignition and liftoff had been in the Huntsville meeting, so it wasn't really my responsibility to point out something wrong with the booster—namely, having people in it!

But had I expressed my opinion in stronger terms, maybe someone would have paid more attention. Unfortunately, we were still trying to stay ahead of the Russians, so there was undue haste in rushing the space shuttle construction process. The haste in putting together the reusable shuttle that had crew and cargo together exacerbated the dangerous situation. They didn't have room for the fuel, so they put the fuel in a separate tank and then had to boost it with solid rockets, one of which failed and caused the *Challenger* accident. The same configuration contributed to the ice that broke off and hit the wing on the *Columbia,* causing another tragic accident.

I had expressed my concerns on these issues with NASA many months before the *Challenger* and *Columbia* tragedies, but NASA gave me the impression that they weren't interested in my ideas for improving the system, so I let it drop.

I was living in California on February 1, 2003, when the *Columbia* space shuttle was scheduled to return from the International Space Station. I had penciled onto my handwritten calendar (remember those?) that the *Columbia* was to land at the Kennedy Space Center at 9 a.m. (EST). As I watched the return coverage on television, I noticed that the radio transmissions from the shuttle suddenly fell silent. That was highly unusual. Ordinarily, there are almost continuous communications back and forth between the ground and the returning spacecraft. Instinctively, I knew that was bad news. Within minutes, all the major television networks broadcast what I feared: The *Columbia* had blown apart.

Actually, the catastrophe was much worse than a normal plane crash. Apparently, the shuttle had been damaged shortly after launch when a piece of foam insulation broke off from the main propellant tank, striking the left wing and damaging *Columbia*'s thermal insulation system, which protects it from temperatures of 3,000 degrees Fahrenheit generated during reentry. Consequently, almost immediately after the *Columbia* reentered Earth's atmosphere, the shuttle began to break apart and disintegrate as it streaked above Texas, spreading bits and pieces of debris across Texas, Arkansas, and Louisiana. All seven crew members died in the catastrophe.

I was deeply grieved by the shuttle accidents. I've often wondered if I could have made a difference had I voiced my concerns over certain elements of the program. Could I have saved the lives of our astronauts had I spoken up in stronger terms? I was confident in my positions; I felt strongly that I was right, but I didn't want to rock the boat. So I went with the flow, gave in to the consensus of opinion, shut my mouth—well, as much as I could—and remained politically correct. Following the shuttle accidents, I made a promise to myself that I would never make that sort of mistake again. If I feel strongly about a matter—especially one that could make the difference between life and death—I am going to speak up, loudly and often.

AFTER I SPENT SOME TIME AS commander at the test pilot school in California, I decided to get back to what I loved—thinking about and designing mission plans that would help NASA recover after the two shuttle accidents. I felt strongly that instead of simply flying missions to the International Space Station, we should continue exploration programs.

As devastating as the space shuttle accidents were, as a nation and as individuals, we had to get back on our feet and begin moving forward again. Eventually, we finished the space station, eliminated the orbiter, and moved to dependence on others to let us hitch a ride up to the orbiting lab that many dedicated American engineers had created and that millions of American tax dollars had financed. Although exploration has continued, our progress has slowed significantly, but I have hope that with a new generation of space enthusiasts coming along, we will soon be going where no one has ever gone before, and we will have learned from our tragic past failures.

Have you ever seen an eagle react when a storm comes up? To escape the tumult, an eagle will purposely fly higher until it is above the turbulence. For an eagle, storms, setbacks, or failures are simply opportunities to go to a higher level. In the same way, you cannot allow the storms of life to hold you down or cause you to live in fear. Usually, fear—especially fear of failure—is the greatest enemy keeping you from getting where you want to go. Fear paralyzes in many ways, but especially if it keeps you from responding wisely and intelligently to challenges. The only way to overcome your fears is to face them head-on.

Just because you face your fears, however, doesn't mean you won't mess up. I discovered that the hard way when I received an invitation from a friend to speak at a gala fundraiser for an animal rights and rescue group in London. I fretted about it and whined to Christina that I really didn't have a message for such a group.

"Of course, you do," Christina said. "Just tell them about how much your family has always enjoyed animals."

"Okay, I can do that." I accepted the invitation.

As background to this story, you need to know that my life has been full of all kinds of interactions with animals. From its inception, NASA was known for rigorous training of its astronauts, but beginning with the Gemini program, the preparation program became more extensive. Not only did we have to study aerodynamics, physics, geology, astronomy, and navigation, and practice exercises designed to simulate weightlessness, but we prepared as much as we could for every possible scenario we might encounter in space and upon landing. We spent long hours practicing for emergencies that we hoped would never happen, but we needed to know what to do should such hazards or even catastrophes occur. Some of the training was somber, some was extremely difficult, and some was actually fun!

We did survival training in the hot Nevada desert, as well as in the sweltering rain forest jungles of Panama and in parts of South America, in case our reentry spacecraft landed off course when we returned to Earth. We learned how to escape a sinking space capsule in case we encountered a problem after splashdown, how to use our parachutes as clothing, as well as how to build makeshift shelters under the worst conditions and to live off the land or sea.

I discovered that I could stay alive in the jungle by catching an iguana and eating small chunks of its claws each day, while keeping the iguana alive and wrapped around my neck. I thought this was a rather ingenious way of maintaining my food supply in the rain forest. Iguana and boa constrictor— sometimes cooked, sometimes not—were actually quite tasty. If you are thinking of the "survivor" shows on television, multiply that exponentially and you will come close to understanding astronaut survival training.

At the same time, my family and I have always loved animals of every kind. My oldest son, Mike, was an avid animal lover, too, and my daughter Jan owned an Appaloosa horse. My younger son, Andy, never saw a dog that he didn't want to bring home. When my family and I moved to a new home after I had returned from the Moon, we purposely purchased property where we could have a variety of animals. Dogs, cats, goats, "rolling" trained pigeons, sheep, chickens, and of course, Jan's horse, all roamed freely around our backyard. We had a barn with two stalls—one for the horse and one for the chickens. We once even had a monkey that we had rescued and brought home with us.

We should have had a sign in our yard that read, "Animals 'R' Us." I love animals!

Unfortunately, during the gala in London, I got so swept up in the moment that I forgot who I was addressing. When I launched into a story about staying alive by nibbling pieces of an iguana, to say they were not impressed would be a gross understatement. More precisely, they were outraged! They didn't care that I had been an animal lover all my life, or that I had walked on the Moon, or anything else. They were ready to have *my* hide!

I apologized as best I could and then made a hasty exit. It was not my finest hour. It was the last time that group invited me to their parties, but I've certainly been invited to many a gala since. Hey, we're all human, and we all make mistakes. When you do, don't make a big deal about it. Apologize, do whatever you can to make it right, and keep moving on.

☾

I'VE ALWAYS BEEN SMART. God blessed me with a good mind and the ability to understand certain things that others have trouble comprehending. But there is a big difference between being smart and being a smart-ass. For most of my life, I've been both.

As any of my family members or my fellow astronauts will tell you, I've always had a healthy dose of self-esteem and an appreciation of my abilities. I tend to say whatever I'm thinking, with few filters, and I'm not bashful about what I believe and don't believe. Moreover, I don't have much patience with incompetence or mental laziness.

These traits have served me well over the years. But there have been times—I know this is hard for some people to believe—when I might have come across as arrogant, stubborn, inflexibly opinionated, and totally devoid of tact.

Someone asked me recently, "Buzz, have you ever said the words, 'I was wrong'?"

"No," I answered without a moment of hesitation. But I might have been wrong about that.

Still, people who know me recognize that I have unusual talents, and I know it, too. The danger, of course, is that my greatest strengths could also reveal my most serious flaws, and sometimes I didn't realize that.

During Gemini 9, Jim Lovell and I were the backup crew, so we were in Mission Control during the launch. Once it appeared that everything was going well and the crew was on their way, Jim and I were no long needed, so I left. On the way home, I stopped off to have a drink, which led to several drinks. Meanwhile, little did I know that Gemini 9 had developed a problem in the "Angry Alligator," a crucial part of the vehicle's docking mechanism necessary for it to complete its mission.

When I heard that the crew was in trouble, I hurried back to Mission Control. I walked into the control room and found everyone anxious and on edge, trying desperately to come up with a solution.

I knew there were wire cutters on board Gemini 9, so I made a suggestion that one of the astronauts do a space walk outside the spacecraft and use the wire cutters to cut the cables to release the Angry Alligator and get it to unlock. I knew that time was of the essence and that the system worked on hydraulics, so if the cable could be released, it might be a quick solution. Unfortunately, perhaps because of my semi-inebriated condition, my suggestion didn't make much sense to my superiors.

When the problem was finally solved, Deke Slayton, one of the original NASA astronauts and now director of flight crew operations, expressed his fury with me. "Buzz, your irresponsible suggestion really irritated me," Deke said.

Bob Gilruth, the program director, echoed Deke's sentiments. "I'm thinking of taking you off the program," Bob railed. Bob was not merely threatening to kick me off the Gemini program; he was talking about kicking me completely out of the space program. This was a big deal and could have derailed my entire career and changed the course of my life.

Deke and Bob thought that I was being reckless in regard to the lives of my fellow astronauts. I really wasn't. I was trying to be helpful. I was searching my mind for a quick solution, and the option I presented made perfectly good sense to me.

Fortunately, Neil Armstrong stood up for me and suggested that I was merely trying to think outside the box to get the Alligator to unlock, and my superiors forgave me . . . after I apologized about a million times.

Sometimes, you have to be big enough to admit when you are wrong—even if you really aren't. What difference does it make who is right or wrong if you allow your conflict to drive a wedge between you and your peers, or you and your loved ones?

(

I'M FREQUENTLY ASKED, "Buzz, what was the scariest thing you experienced in space?" I have a ready answer, because it reminds me of another mistake I made that could have been costly.

After blasting off the Moon, our next challenge was to successfully rendezvous the *Eagle* with Mike Collins and the *Columbia* command module that we hoped would return us to Earth. Our rendezvous plan was not a straight shot off the lunar surface to intersect the *Columbia*. Instead, Neil and I orbited the Moon for a couple of hours, and during our second orbit of the Moon, the *Columbia* came into sight. We had practiced docking one spacecraft to another in simulations, and U.S. astronauts had successfully performed the procedure as early as the Gemini program, so we had a well-established plan.

But as Neil and I approached the *Columbia* to initiate the connecting/docking procedures, although I knew our flight checklist said one thing, I had a spur-of-the-moment idea to dock in a slightly different manner, in a way that I thought might make docking the two spacecraft much easier. Rather than guiding the *Eagle* into a straight-ahead approach with the *Columbia*, I suggested to Neil that we use a rolling-and-pitching approach different from the direct horizontal line we had anticipated and practiced.

Neil agreed, and nobody at Mission Control raised any objections, so we initiated the unrehearsed procedures. As it turned out, the rolling-and-pitching approach was not a good thing to do, because it caused the platform to become locked, and we were not able to use the *Eagle*'s primary thrusters, the main means of guidance, to control the spacecraft through its final few feet to dock with the *Columbia.*

Can you imagine that? After successfully landing on the Moon and spending a few hours exploring its surface, then successfully launching off the Moon and rendezvousing with our ride home, we nearly blew the whole deal because of my last-minute idea to break away from tried-and-tested procedures.

I had suggested to my commander that we do things differently, and that was my mistake. It was his mistake to assume that I knew what I was talking about! So we both made mistakes—brought about by me!

We recovered using the "abort guidance" system to bring the *Eagle* into proper alignment for docking with the *Columbia.*

Neither Neil nor I said anything about our potentially mission-destroying goof, although I'm sure the rendezvous experts at Mission Control in Houston knew what had happened. They were probably going nuts as they watched their computer screens. They graciously didn't squeal on us. Maybe they thought, *Well, Buzz is Dr. Rendezvous. Surely, he knows what he is doing.*

Once we corrected our docking plans, the rendezvous occurred just as I had imagined it years earlier when I had developed my theories and techniques for manned spacecraft rendezvous. It was picture-perfect. Four hours after Neil and I left the lunar surface, I heard one of the sweetest sounds I'd ever heard—the latches locking shut as Mike threw the switches inside the command module to secure the *Eagle* to the *Columbia*. The three of us were together again, and soon we'd be on our way home.

You may not always be right; you may not always win, but you won't know if you don't try, and you won't have a chance to win if you don't take the shot. Make a decision; if it is wrong, correct it if possible, learn from it, and move on. But whatever you do, don't allow the fear of failure to paralyze you.

Yes, failure is always an option. You may fail at times; you may fall flat on your face. But get back up, brush off the dust, and keep pushing the boundaries; keep pushing yourself to go outside your own comfort zone. Don't allow mistakes, disappointment, rejection, or failure to define you. Despite your flaws, flub-ups, or failures, don't let "disappointment" or "rejection" be the final words.

When I was a high school student, I aspired to become a Rhodes scholar and to attend Oxford University in England. To me, that was the epitome of academic achievement. I applied twice but wasn't accepted as a Rhodes scholar, so I went on to West Point and later to MIT instead, where I received my master's degree and continued with my doctoral studies. I completed my doctoral thesis on the subject of "space rendezvous." That failure to become a Rhodes scholar made all the difference in the world for me and for a lot of other people.

Recently, I was in England and had the opportunity to visit Oxford. I smiled as I thought of myself as a jolly old English academic. My life, and perhaps America's space program, may have been dramatically different had I not failed to become a Rhodes scholar.

Disappointments come at every age and at every level of success. For instance, I was disappointed after the successful mission of Apollo 11, when I was not appointed as commandant of the Air Force Academy in Colorado. That was a position in which I felt I could thrive.

Shortly after Neil, Mike, and I completed a world tour following Apollo 11, we met with President Richard Nixon at the White House for a private dinner. The president asked each of us what we'd like to do in the future. "I know you've been talking with Secretary Rogers," he said, looking at Mike, "about a position with the State Department."

"Yes, sir," Mike agreed. "I'm looking forward to that."

I was a bit surprised when Neil answered the president's query about his future plans. "I'd like to stay with NASA for a while," Neil said, "and maybe work in the aeronautics department." I was somewhat surprised that the first man ever to walk on another celestial body did not want to work in the space program, but wanted to return to aviation. I didn't fault him for that. Neil had always loved being a test pilot.

When the president turned to me and asked about my future plans, I didn't know what to tell him. I was thinking about returning to the Air Force. As an astronaut who had walked on the Moon, I could see myself as a motivator and a role model for young airmen at the Air Force Academy, and that position appealed to me. But for some reason, I couldn't bring myself to suggest it to President Nixon. I guess I should have, because by the time I asked to be released from NASA to return to the Air Force in June 1971, the position of commandant of the Air Force Academy was already filled by the son of the legendary Air Force general Hoyt Vandenberg.

Instead, I was offered a position at Edwards Air Force Base in California, where I became commandant of the USAF Test Pilot School, a great job, but I cut my aeronautical teeth as a fighter pilot; I had never even been a test pilot.

Not surprisingly, I commanded the test pilots' school for only nine months—admittedly, nine of the most stressful months of my life—before deciding to retire from the Air Force. I was only 42 years of age, with no real exciting job opportunities presenting themselves. But to me, the strain on my emotions and on all of my family relationships was no longer worth the struggle. I was not about to let "rejection" and "failure" be the final words of my life.

(

I'VE SINCE LEARNED THAT I MUST transform pain to power if I want to overcome setbacks. And sometimes that means I simply choose to ignore something that I don't like. Even in the little things, the inconsequential or seemingly insignificant, I've learned to grin and bear it. For instance, for years, my wife made me the same Cobb salad every day, complete with veggies, boiled eggs, and fat-free mayonnaise. Unless we were going out to eat someplace, I knew what I could expect.

After my wife and I divorced, Christina carried on the tradition of making me a huge salad for lunch every day. Of course, she followed the example she had seen, including all the ingredients she had seen me eating for years, filling up the bowl with all sorts of vegetables, including carrots and celery sticks.

One day Christina came in as I was finishing up my salad, and I said to her, "You know, when I was a kid, I always hated celery."

"Oh? And you like it now?"

"Naaah, I still hate it."

"What?" Christina asked in surprise. "Where is it? Did you take it out of your salad?"

"No, I ate it."

"Why?" she asked.

"Because that was my West Point training. We were taught to eat everything on our plates and not complain about it."

Sure, there are some things in life that are hard to swallow, but if you just gulp hard, you can get it down and keep on going. You have to believe there is some coconut ice cream—my favorite—out there somewhere, and that good things will be coming along soon!

# CHAPTER EIGHT

# PRACTICE RESPECT FOR ALL PEOPLE.

Differences in race, religion, politics, sexual orientation, or other barriers that seem to divide some people have never greatly affected my regard for another person. My son Andy jokes that to me there are only two kinds of people in this world—those who are interested in space, and those who aren't. Andy is not far from wrong, but he's not quite right, either.

None of us has a right to be a snob, regardless of who you are or what you have accomplished. No human being has a license to be disrespectful to another person. Regardless of another person's race, religion, financial status, or outward appearances, acknowledge that we are all on this planet together, and despite our personality differences, we are pretty much the same. We all put on our pants the same way, unless you happen to hold yours out and jump into them.

So don't judge.

When I was growing up, I could usually determine if a person was important or successful by the way he or she dressed. Whether the person was a schoolteacher, the president of a company, or a Hollywood star was relatively easy to discern, because most complied with the accepted norms of "dress for success." Successful businessmen, for example, tended to wear dark suits with white shirts and either red, blue, or yellow "power ties." Those days are long gone. It is especially precarious nowadays to judge people by their clothing or external appearance. Today you may meet a multimillionaire or a computer genius dressed in baggy pants or jeans with holes in them, wearing a T-shirt or sweatshirt. You never know.

One time, I was on my way back from a large event in Arkansas, and Christina and I were seated at the airport awaiting our flight home. Several people recognized me and wanted to talk with me, but Christina ran interference, informing them that I had been keeping a grueling schedule and was fatigued, so it might not be the best time for a conversation.

"I'm going to run to the restroom before we leave," Christina informed me, vacating the seat next to mine.

"Okay, fine," I said. "I'll just sit right here and wait for you."

"Don't get into any trouble while I'm gone," she warned me facetiously.

"Who, me?" I feigned shock.

Christina rolled her eyes and headed to the restroom. She

had no sooner walked away when another young woman approached and sat down in the seat next to me. I guessed her to be around 19 years of age, and she sported bloodred dreadlocks in her hair and piercings all over her head and body, and carried several brightly colored translucent Hula-Hoops that seemed to have lights inside them.

She didn't seem to recognize me, and she looked rather ratty in her appearance, but I was fascinated by her Hula-Hoops, so I struck up a conversation with her. "Why are you carrying those hoops?" I asked.

"Oh, I'm a performance artist and I use them in my show. They light up as I move."

"They light up?" She had my full attention.

"Yeah, watch," she offered. "I'll show you." She swung several of the hoops around her waist and arms and began to move her hips. The hoops swirled around her and lit up like a Christmas tree. I was impressed.

She sat back down and we talked further. She told me that she was on her way to Australia to attend school.

"Are you going to do any scuba diving while you are there?" I asked.

"Oh, I'd love to scuba dive in Australia," she said.

I knew I had found a kindred spirit, regardless of her unusual looks and occupation. In my peripheral vision, I noticed several onlookers scowling at us incredulously, as though saying, "What is he doing talking to *her?*"

I didn't care. She was an interesting person and I'm always interested in interesting people.

Christina returned, and I introduced her to the dreadlocked young woman. "And look," I said, "she has Hula-Hoops!"

"Uh-huh," Christina responded cautiously. "Hula-Hoops?"

"Yes, and they light up!"

"I see," Christina said. "We'll be boarding soon, Buzz." She smiled at the strange-looking young woman and sat down across from us, while the red-dreads girl and I continued our conversation. Christina seemed to be working on her phone, occasionally pointing it in my direction.

Before long, it was time for the first-class passengers to board, so we said goodbye to the young woman. Upon entering the airplane, as is my usual practice, I stopped to chat with the pilots, greeting them as one pilot to another, asking them questions and engaging them in conversation about flying. Christina went on to our seats.

The young woman with the red dreads was one of the last passengers to get on the plane. As the young woman passed by our seats in first class, on her way to coach seating, Christina stopped her. "I took a few pictures of you and Buzz," she said. "Would you mind if I send them out on Twitter?"

"I'm not on Twitter," the red-dreads woman said, "but I don't care. Send whatever you want."

"Okay, the pictures will be on our website. Do you know who he is?"

"I don't know; he said his name is Buzz."

"Yes, that's right," Christina said. "*Buzz Aldrin,* as in Buzz Aldrin of Apollo 11, the guy who walked on the Moon."

"Holy crap," the girl blurted.

"Do you have any idea how lucky you are to be able to talk to Buzz Aldrin for so long?" one of her fellow passengers asked. She had no idea. Nor did she care. And nor did I.

By then, everyone in first class was listening to their conversation—and they began applauding.

(

I TRY TO TREAT EVERY PERSON WITH DIGNITY and respect, whether that person is the president of the United States—all of whom I have met since Richard Nixon—or Queen Elizabeth of England or a waitress at a local restaurant. In fact, you can tell a lot about another person you are considering as a business partner or a marriage partner simply by observing the way that person treats an individual who is serving them. When people are rude or inconsiderate or treat waitstaff as inanimate robots that exist and function merely for their convenience, service, or pleasure, you can be sure those people will eventually treat your customers or you in a similar manner at some point.

I try to treat a janitor with the same respect I give to the CEO of a company. Why? Because every human being deserves our respect and deserves to be treated with dignity.

Treating children with respect is also a big deal to me. Part of the reason I respect kids' curiosity so much is because I was a curious and adventurous child myself. During my early childhood, my family lived in a large house in Montclair, New Jersey, and the home had some secret passageways. I loved exploring those passageways, even though a few times, I nearly got stuck in one of them.

About the time I was eight years old, I had my own room on the third floor of the house. In good weather, at night I often climbed out a window onto the porch roof from the third floor and looked up at the stars . . . dreaming of what it might be like to travel there.

I was also fascinated by scuba diving at an early age and was intrigued by how the equipment worked. I had seen a cartoon strip in which the heroes were trying to escape from some marauders. They jumped into a lake and kept their heads underwater, using bamboo shoots to facilitate their breathing as they hid from their pursuers. When I saw that cartoon, I figured that I would experiment and try it out.

I found a hose and used it to breathe as I went underwater. Unfortunately, as I got deeper below the surface, I quickly realized that my lungs couldn't handle the pressure without having proper oxygen. I nearly drowned! Gurgling and choking, I popped up out of the water, thinking, *That trick the heroes did in the cartoon is not possible!*

After World War II broke out, I kept a large map of the world in my room, and I kept track of air raids and bombings by following the newsreels. Even then, I was curious.

When a child asks me a question, I don't ignore it. Nor do I attempt to "dumb down" the answer; I simplify my response and may not include a lot of technical details, but I respect the child's intelligence and encourage his or her inquisitiveness.

When talking with children, I like to get down on their level, so I will kneel or stoop or even sit on the floor so I can look into their eyes. I ask questions and I listen carefully to their answers, taking my time, and giving them my full attention. I never speak to children in a condescending manner, and I welcome every question. Kids love to talk about space or underwater exploration, and I love sharing my experiences with them.

Recently, a little girl asked me, "Do you have to be brave to go into space?"

"No," I told her with a smile. "You just have to be smart."

# CHAPTER NINE

# DO WHAT YOU BELIEVE IS RIGHT EVEN WHEN OTHERS CHOOSE OTHERWISE.

Always maintain your honesty and integrity even if people around you compromise theirs.

Making tough decisions may often set you apart, and put you a bit out of sync with your peers. Let's be honest: Taking the high road when people around you are willing to compromise what is right may not always draw kudos from your friends or peers. But what they think of you is not the paramount issue. You want to be able to live with yourself, knowing that you are not perfect but that you are committed to doing the right thing as best you can. That's not as easy as it sounds, as I discovered when I was a cadet at the United States Military Academy at West Point, one of our nation's most prestigious military institutions.

In 1947 as a high school senior, 17 years of age, I received an offer of a full-ride scholarship to MIT, my father's alma mater. I turned it down because I was also honored to receive an appointment to West Point, and that commitment to serve my country has colored everything in my life. Wealth and fame have never been strong motivations for me, although I have been blessed—or cursed, depending on your perspective—with both. Making a fortune in the stock market never mattered to me, nor did having an abundance of expensive material possessions, though I've enjoyed some of those. My goal has always been to serve my country with honor and distinction. That's why I went to West Point, and that's why I went to the Moon.

During the summer of 2015, Christina ran across my "travel vouchers" for the Apollo 11 trip to the Moon. There it was, listing as "points of travel":

> FROM Houston, Texas
> TO Cape Kennedy, Florida
>   Moon
>   Pacific Ocean (U.S.S. *Hornet*)
>   Hawaii
> and return to Houston, Texas

Christina was astounded that NASA paid me only $33.31 for travel expenses. My only reimbursement request was for a rental car that I used prior to launch. After a journey of more than half a million miles, that was the only travel expense that I listed, so that's what NASA repaid me. "Government meals and quarters furnished for all the above dates," the voucher states: July 7 through July 27, including the period from July 19 (1325 hours, arrived at Moon) to July 21 (2400 hours, left Moon).

Similarly, Neil Armstrong, Mike Collins, and I had to fill out a U.S. Customs form upon our return from the Moon. My customs declaration form stated *"Departure from:* Moon. *Arrival at:* Honolulu, Hawaii, U.S.A. *Cargo, items to declare:* Moon rocks, Moon dust samples." Then in a rather cryptic note, the form included the statement, *"Any other condition on board which may lead to the spread of disease? To be determined"*—because it was unknown what health impact our adventure on the lunar surface might eventually have on our bodies. Neil, Mike, and I all signed the official declaration document, as did the local customs agent in Hawaii. To me, going to the Moon was merely an extension of the commitment I had made to serve my country years earlier.

When I said the words of the oath at West Point, "Duty, honor, country, and service," I meant them, and I still embrace them to this day. I made the commitment not simply to enlist for a few years but to serve my country for the rest of my life. And I am proud to have done so. Serving my country has been the greatest honor of my life.

At West Point, I took seriously the high standards by which all cadets promised to live and operate. The academy upheld a simple but strict honor code: "A cadet will not lie, cheat, steal, or tolerate those who do." Not only were cadets expected to do their own work, never compromising their own integrity, they were also required to report anyone else who might be cheating. The "honor code" at West Point meant that an instructor could literally leave a room while administering a test and expect that the cadets would not share answers, copy someone else's paper, or do anything that might skew the results. The honor code, although adhered to and administered by the commandant of the academy as well as the superintendent of the academy, was basically peer enforced, cadets keeping each other accountable.

West Point had such confidence in the willingness of cadets to adhere to the honor code, the academy had set up an almost irresistible temptation—dividing the corps of cadets into two regiments, meeting on two separate days, with both taking identical classes and receiving identical tests. For instance, one class might take a test on Monday, and the other received that same test on Wednesday; in the meantime, the cadets were expected not to discuss the contents of the exam, much less the answers to questions. That usually worked well, but in situations where members of the two regiments mixed, especially on the athletic teams, inevitably the temptation to ask, "What was on the test?" proved too hard to resist and the program was compromised.

Nowadays, many students are accustomed to asking such questions, and there are entire businesses thriving in America that do nothing other than help students prepare for college entrance exams such as the SAT or ACT. Their method is simple and effective, and the businesses help students improve their scores by reviewing previous tests and practicing for the exam, which will most likely be quite similar.

But at West Point in my day, we were expected to do our own work. We didn't ask our fellow cadets, "Hey, what was on the test you took yesterday?" That would be breaking the honor code. A cadet accused of violating the honor code could be sanctioned or possibly expelled from the academy, so pointing out an indiscretion by a fellow cadet was always taken seriously. That's why I faced such a dilemma when I discovered a cadet in my class cheating on an exam.

During an exam my second year at West Point, the instructor left the room. Not surprisingly, the cadets taking the test remained absolutely silent. I was poring over my exam when I momentarily glanced up from my work and noticed one of the most respected cadets at the academy pull out a crib sheet—a piece of paper with answers to the test! I was shocked, but I didn't say anything to him or anyone else at the time. I finished the exam and exited the room, feeling great consternation. What was I to do? I was certain that I had witnessed a cadet cheating on an exam, a blatant violation of the honor code. If I ignored his actions, I would be as guilty as he was, and I knew the code demanded that failure to report a violation could also lead to expulsion. But if I reported his actions, I ran the risk of it being his word against mine.

I grappled with the dilemma for a while, but really the decision about what I had to do was a foregone conclusion for me. I knew that I had to report the cadet I saw cheating.

I went to my honor representative and reported the incident. He went to the cadet's room and found the crib notes he had used during the exam, but unfortunately, the honor representative did not confiscate the notes. He merely saw them. Later, the already graded paper that the cadet had used as crib notes disappeared.

When the case came up before the cadet council, all 24 company representatives of the honor committee concluded that an indiscretion had occurred. But because the representative had not retrieved the crib notes as evidence, lacking any tangible proof of the honor code violation, the situation came down to my word against that of the accused cadet. As part of his defense, he implied that I was the one cheating, and that I was jealous of him, so I had lied about him cheating. Of course, nothing could have been further from the truth.

In similar situations at West Point, if a cadet was accused of an indiscretion yet there was not enough evidence to prove it, the cadet in question was "silenced"—ostracized and shunned. A borderline statement that was evasive was known as "quibbling"—dodging the issue and covering an honor violation. But when I reported the cheating incident, the commandant refused to allow the cadet in question to be silenced. Perhaps because of the cadet's popularity, he was able to weather the storm, and he was never shunned. In fact, the man involved went on to become a decorated general; I went to war in Korea.

As it turned out, the incident that I had witnessed was only the tip of the iceberg. The following year, 90 cadets were dismissed from West Point for cheating, including our star quarterback and 36 other members of the Army football team. It was one of the largest scandals ever to rock a U.S. military academy.

Thanks to round-the-clock news coverage, as well as social media covering the latest scandal or public indiscretions nowadays, most of us barely blink when we are informed of another sordid mess involving a public official, a military officer, or even a minister. But in the late 1940s and early 1950s, such breaches of integrity and other "moral failures" were considered serious matters, especially at our nation's military academies.

I graduated third in my class at West Point in 1951, but reporting the cheater cost me some good friendships and, no doubt, some good future connections. Nevertheless, I never regretted doing the right thing. Some people might say, "But Buzz, what's the use of being honest if the cheater goes free and you are the one who suffers?"

I didn't see it that way, and I didn't want to back away from West Point's strict honor principles, nor did many others at the academy. Moreover, some recognized that I respected the rules of the academy, and that I could be trusted. That paid huge dividends in my future.

(

YEARS LATER, WHILE STANDING ON the lunar surface, Neil Armstrong and I were informed that someone wanted to speak with us. The next voice we heard said, "Hello, Neil and Buzz. I'm talking to you from the Oval Room[Office] of the White House, and this certainly has to be the most historic telephone call ever made from the White House."

Neil and I paused our activity and listened as the president of the United States, Richard M. Nixon, talked to us "long-distance" and expressed congratulations and the pride of America.

"I just can't tell you how proud we all are of what you have done," the president said. "For every American, this has to be the proudest day of our lives, and for people all over the world, I am sure that they, too, join with Americans in recognizing what an immense feat this is. Because of what you have done, the heavens have become a part of man's world, and as you talk to us from the Sea of Tranquility, it inspires us to redouble our efforts to bring peace and tranquility to Earth. For one priceless moment in the whole history of man, all the people on this Earth are truly one—one in their pride in what you have done and one in our prayers that you will return safely to Earth."

"Thank you, Mr. President," Neil said into his helmet microphone, his words transmitted back to Earth and around the globe. "It is a great honor and privilege for us to be here representing not only the United States, but men of peaceable nations, men with an interest and a curiosity, and men with a vision for the future. It is an honor for us to be able to participate here today."

We talked briefly with the president, and then Neil and I went back to work. Hearing from our president while we were on the lunar surface was a special surprise, but I'm sure glad I didn't have to pay for that phone call!

(

OF COURSE, NOT EVERYBODY ON EARTH was as excited about our achievement as was President Nixon. It was a time in our nation's history when patriotism was out of style for certain factions. But doing the right thing means that you cannot allow the foolish or ignorant ideas, actions, or attitudes of others to deter you from your destiny or force you off your determined path. So the response of a few protestors didn't matter to me.

After landing on the Moon, Neil, Mike, and I were kept in quarantine for 21 days so doctors and scientists could study us, just in case we brought back some unusual germs from our time in space. As silly as it seems now, there was serious concern that we might contract something alien that could affect life on Earth. That may seem far-fetched, but keep in mind that travelers from Hawaii to California are not permitted to transport certain fruits and flowers from the islands to the mainland, because certain fruit flies could devastate California's crops. Because nobody had ever returned from another celestial body, scientists did not want to take any chances of us transporting something that could be deadly to life on Earth.

When we finally completed our quarantine, my fellow Apollo 11 astronauts and I were treated to a fabulous ticker tape parade in New York. Neil, Mike, and I were doused with what seemed like a blizzard of confetti as our motorcade slowly rolled up Wall Street to Broadway and on to City Hall and the United Nations Building with thousands of people waving, reaching out to us, and cheering in congratulations as we went. When I saw a troop of Boy Scouts in front of us, each one carrying an American flag, it evoked within me an overwhelming sense of patriotism and hope for our future. Then, that same day, we were off to Chicago, where we experienced a similar parade and reception. Mayor Richard J. Daley presented us with a special bowl commemorating our accomplishments. The bowl was stolen before we left town.

Then it was on to Los Angeles where a few hours later, Neil, Mike, and I received another huge reception and were treated like heroes. To close out the long day, we attended a celebration banquet with President Nixon and about 3,000 of his closest friends. In addition to my wife and children, my father attended the event and looked on, beaming, as the president of the United States presented Neil, Mike, and me each with a Medal of Freedom, the highest honor given to civilians in our nation.

Although each of us had spoken briefly at the receptions and celebrations, our first public speaking engagement was on the campus of Marquette University in Milwaukee, Wisconsin, where we were to receive the Père Marquette Discovery Award. We were not prepared for the reception we received. As Neil, Mike, and I made our way from the limousines to the building in which we were to speak, disgruntled students protesting something—I never did find out what—lined the sidewalks and attempted to pelt us with eggs! Fortunately, we were too far away for the eggs to hit their targets, but it was a rude awakening to realize that not everyone was thrilled that we had successfully gone to the Moon and returned to Earth.

To me it was sad that those students were so caught up in their political agendas that they could not support an unprecedented accomplishment that opened new horizons for all humans.

(

WHEN NEIL ARMSTRONG AND I planted the first American flag on the Moon—no easy feat getting a light, hollow pole wedged down into the rock surface that had been pummeled by asteroids for thousands of years—I stepped back and saluted, almost instinctively. Neil took my photo as I did. That salute was one of the proudest moments of my life. Although not given to emotionalism, patriotism and love for my country overwhelmed me. All of my West Point training, my years of service as an Air Force fighter pilot during the Korean War, my time in Germany flying simulated nuclear attack missions, every time I'd ever placed my hand over my heart as I stated the Pledge of Allegiance, every time I'd ever heard "The Star-Spangled Banner"— it was all there, wrapped up in that simple salute on the Moon. And for the record, I've always thought the flag Neil and I placed looked the best of the six flags that were planted on the Moon by astronauts between July 1969 and December 1972, when the Apollo mission was completed.

Doing the right thing isn't always easy—especially when others don't understand or appreciate your actions—but doing the right thing is always worth it in the long run.

# CHAPTER TEN

# TRUST YOUR GUT ...
# AND YOUR INSTRUMENTS.

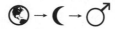

**H**ave you ever been traveling through the darkness in a strange, unknown area, with nothing to guide you but a GPS? You cannot see the road signs—if there are any—and there is nobody around from whom you can obtain accurate directions or other pertinent information. A feeling of loneliness and, worse yet, *aloneness* grips you. You make a turn but you aren't quite sure if it is correct. You nervously try to listen to the mechanical voice talking to you from the GPS, and then you hear that terse statement, "Recalculating." That's bad news because you realize that you have messed up, but it is good news because you know that your onboard guidance system is making adjustments that will help to get you back on the right track.

In some ways, that is similar to traveling in space. You must trust your instruments to get you safely where you plan to go.

But it is not a blind trust, and there are moments, even in space, when you must "trust your gut" and override your instruments as you make a tough course decision on your own.

Prior to landing on the Moon, Neil Armstrong and I practiced on Earth for hours and hours in a simulated lunar landing training vehicle. As the lunar module pilot, I often wondered why I was practicing drills that would obviously never be needed—flying the lunar landing training vehicle. I couldn't imagine any conditions under which Neil might turn over to me the command controls of the lunar landing module. If we experienced a problem that serious, no doubt, we would abort the landing anyhow.

But NASA wanted us to prepare for any possibility, so day after day, I worked alongside Neil. Even in the simulator, though, things could sometimes go wrong. We had several "accidents" in which something caused us to lose directional control and we had to abort during a simulated landing.

Nevertheless, we weren't worried. We knew we could trust our instruments and the engineers who were helping us.

Besides, Neil had plenty of history with close calls. He had experienced several previous crashes, but his courage never wavered, nor did his ability to remain calm under pressure. During the Korean War, he flew from an aircraft carrier, making low-altitude bombing runs aimed at destroying bridges and other infrastructure, but as an antiaircraft measure, the North Koreans strung up wires by which they could trip low-flying planes. The wires were difficult to spot from the air. On one mission, Neil's plane ran through one of these cables, knocking off more than six feet of his right wing. He battled to maintain control of his aircraft, keeping it at high speed to avoid dropping out of the sky. He realized that he could not land on the aircraft carrier and that he would have to bail out, which he did.

Years later, while training as an astronaut, Neil flew home to Ohio and had another accident. It didn't faze him. He literally crashed a plane and went home and had dinner with his family, including a piece of pie for dessert.

During Gemini 8, Neil flew with Dave Scott, and an important part of their mission was to dock with the Agena, an unmanned spacecraft that had been launched earlier that day. The procedure was essential for future rendezvous and docking missions we hoped to do during the Apollo mission. Neil and Dave performed a beautiful docking maneuver but then something went wrong. The spacecraft began rolling, and the astronauts couldn't do anything about it. They were forced to undock the Gemini capsule from the Agena, but that only made things worse. The Gemini went into a rapid roll, practically a tumble, spinning at nearly one revolution a second. There was a strong concern that the astronauts would black out, and that would most likely be deadly.

Neil switched on the reentry system in hopes of regaining control of the spacecraft. During the high-speed roll, Neil was able to reach up and activate the switches that slowly brought the Gemini under control and saved their lives. He rarely talked much about the incident, but it was another close call with death.

On May 6, 1968, more than a year before the flight of Apollo 11, Neil had another close call. Because the lunar lander itself, with its wafer-thin walls, was far too delicate to be used for practice, part of the preparation for landing on the Moon required Neil to practice in the Lunar Landing Research Vehicle, a strange-looking contraption meant to approximate the real module. We derisively referred to the vehicle as the "Flying Bedstead," but it actually flew. It was not easy to control the vehicle, and during a test in which Neil alone was maneuvering the vehicle above a landing strip in Houston, something in the vehicle's fuel system caused the trainer to tilt for some unknown reason. Neil had little more than a second to make a decision. He hit the ejection button just as the training vehicle exploded in the sky and crashed to the runway, totally demolishing it. Neil escaped with a few relatively minor injuries, including a gash in his tongue from his teeth that made it nearly impossible to understand his words for a few days. But he survived.

Despite his numerous accidents, Neil remained unflappable. To him, that's just what test pilots did, and accidents went with the territory. Nothing seemed to shake him. He was just the kind of guy you wanted to be standing next to you as you searched for a place to land on the Moon.

When Neil and I slipped through the tunnel from the *Columbia* to the *Eagle,* it was the first time for either of us to ever fly the thing. Although we had practiced repeatedly on simulators, nobody had ever before tried to land an actual lunar module.

That's why it was a bit disconcerting when the *Eagle*'s computer alarms went off with about six minutes to go during our descent to the Moon. At about 35,000 feet above the surface, a little lower than what the average commercial passenger plane flies, the data screen in front of us went totally blank.

"Program alarm!" Neil reported to Houston.

Something was affecting our guidance computer, overloading its ability to handle the massive amount of data coming into it. Alarms continued going off every few seconds, but even though it took one and a half seconds each way for us to communicate with Mission Control, we had to trust the guys on Earth when they told us it was safe to proceed for a landing.

*Trust your instruments.* At about 2,000 feet above the surface, another alarm lit up. Another quick check with Houston told us to keep going. Neil was looking out the window, searching for a good spot to land, while my eyes were glued to the altimeter readings. With our communications dropouts and computer glitches, if we were going to come down in one piece, he needed accurate readings.

"Seven-fifty," I called out to Neil, letting him know that we were 750 feet above the surface while he continued to scan the surface intently.

"Pretty rocky," Neil said.

"Six hundred," I said.

*But also trust your gut.*

At only 600 feet above the surface, Neil switched over to manual controls, taking our lives into his own hands, as we tried to find a safe place to land before we ran out of fuel. It was a classic instance of "Trust your instruments, but also trust your gut."

"Forty feet," I said. "Picking up some dust."

"Thirty seconds," Charlie Duke, our Mission Control liaison, said from Earth, letting us know that we had only 30 seconds of fuel left before we crashed.

Neil slowed the *Eagle* even more, just as he had the Lunar Landing Research Vehicle from which he had to eject 14 months earlier, but there was no ejection possible for us on the *Eagle*.

That's when I saw it—the shadow of one of our three footpads, which had touched the Moon's surface. "Contact light," I said.

The *Eagle* settled onto the surface of the Moon. We had less than 20 seconds of fuel left, but we had made it.

Whether you are trying to land on the Moon or land a new job, it is important to have a game plan you trust and stick with it. But it is equally important, at times, to trust your own inner direction, and to control your own destiny by the choices you make.

( 

OF COURSE, IT IS ALSO HELPFUL TO remember that some things aren't always as they seem. I once did a television interview for a show with a new hip interviewer who the producers said was trying to relate to young people, an interviewer with whom I was not familiar, for the *Da Ali G Show*. I had no idea that the interviewer, Ali G, was actually a character created by British comedian Sacha Baron Cohen. The interviewer showed up at my home wearing a bright yellow floor-length robe, which should have tipped me off, but I've done interviews with people all around the world, so I simply assumed he was from some part of Africa or India, because he had a British accent. During the interview, I was repeatedly perplexed by the unusual and ridiculous questions he asked, such as "What was it like not being the first man on the Moon? Were you ever jealous of Louis Armstrong?" I patiently explained to him that my fellow Moonwalker was *Neil* Armstrong. Later, I clarified to the interviewer that it was actually the Moon on which I had walked, not the Sun. Cohen never broke from his character, and I did the entire interview thinking it was absolutely real.

Things aren't always as they seem. Today, when I see clips of that interview, I crack up laughing.

☾

WHEN NEIL, MIKE, AND I SPLASHED down in the Pacific Ocean, the recovery team wiped us down thoroughly with an iodine solution to decontaminate us, because NASA was concerned about us bringing back strange bacteria or germs from the Moon dust we had encountered. Before boarding the U.S.S. *Hornet,* the ship that would carry us to Hawaii, we quickly suited up with biological isolation garments (BIG) suits—similar to modern-day hazmat (hazardous materials) outfits—including gas mask–type respirators over our faces, until we could be transferred to a specially made quarantine unit aboard the ship. It has always struck me as odd that the recovery guys took the rags they used to wipe us off and dropped them into the ocean! I guess they figured the poor underwater creatures could fend for themselves. Who knows? Maybe our Moon germs spawned a whole new breed of Godzilla movies!

Again, because nobody knew what effects the Moon dust might have on human beings, NASA was taking no chances. Once inside the quarantine unit, a specially adapted Airstream trailer, we were able to remove the BIG suits and move around in normal uniforms or other clothing. Still, we were kept in an airtight isolation unit. The three of us peeked out a window with a speaker, similar to a window at a movie theater, when President Nixon came to visit us and stood outside the quarantine unit, talking to us from behind the glass.

Our entire quarantine unit was flown from Hawaii, where the *Hornet* dropped us off, all the way back to Houston, with us still in it! We spent the next three weeks inside the quarantine unit being observed like mice in a cage. The unit was comfortable, but there was little to do and nowhere to go, so we got bored in a hurry.

One day, I was sitting at the table staring at the floor, and I noticed a small crack in the middle of the floor, with tiny ants coming up through it! *Hmm, I guess this thing isn't really tightly sealed,* I thought. Imagine, if we had brought some sort of alien substance back with us, those ants could have contracted it and taken it back out to the world!

Things aren't always as they seem.

On the way to the Moon, about three days and 200,000 miles into the journey, I noticed something odd-looking outside our window. It appeared to be a light or an object following alongside us in space! Neil and Mike saw it as well.

It was something outside our window that was close enough to be observed, so of course, we wondered what it could be.

Certainly, we could see all sorts of stars outside, but traveling along close to us was this mysterious object. We could see it, but we couldn't identify what it was, so in that sense, whatever it was, I suppose it could technically be described as an "unidentified flying object."

Mike thought he could see the object with a telescope. When it was in one position, it looked like a series of ellipses, but when he looked at it from another, sharper view, it looked more L-shaped, so that didn't tell us very much.

We were wary but nonetheless reluctant to blurt, "Hey, Houston, we have something moving along beside us, and we don't know what it is. Can you tell us what that might be?"

We knew our transmissions were being heard not only by Mission Control, but by millions of other people as well. We were four-fifths of the way to our goal; we certainly didn't want to endanger our mission or have to turn back now because somebody might be afraid that we would encounter aliens.

Neil calmly spoke to Mission Control, "Houston, do you have any idea where the S-IV-B is with respect to us?" The S-IV-B was the final stage of the rocket that had been jettisoned two days earlier, several hours after we had launched from Cape Canaveral, when we had made a midcourse correction that sent us off in the direction of the Moon. On later missions, that stage of the rocket would be sent crashing into the Moon so scientists could study the seismic effects, but on our mission, the discarded rocket made an evasive move to miss the Moon and continued on its way toward the Sun.

Houston reported back to us, "The S-IV-B is about 6,000 nautical miles from you. Over."

Hmm, 6,000 miles away? If that was so, then what we were seeing couldn't be the discarded fourth stage of our rocket. We didn't think that the object following us was that far away, but we decided that because we could do nothing, we might as well go to sleep and not worry about it.

Of course, people who are convinced that aliens and extra-terrestrials exist contend that we were being tracked by a UFO. It certainly *seemed* that way.

NASA encouraged Neil, Mike, and me not to talk about the strange object we saw in space for fear of public ridicule. We tacitly agreed, and despite the hopes of people wanting us to confirm the existence of a UFO, we kept our comments to ourselves. But we all knew that we saw *something!*

So if three fairly intelligent human beings, all of whom had flown in space previously, agreed that we saw something outside our window, something that appeared to be a UFO, that should be evidence enough for the existence of UFOs, right?

Not necessarily. Remember, things aren't always as they seem.

All sorts of suggestions have been posed to explain the unidentified flying object that we three Apollo 11 astronauts saw with our own eyes. Some have even suggested that it was another spacecraft, sent up by Russia to keep an eye on us around the same time as our mission. That was ridiculous. How Russia could launch a rocket to the Moon without our noticing is totally incomprehensible to me.

Ruling out the outrageous possibility that we were being followed by a spacecraft from another country, we were left to believe that the object we saw was either the jettisoned S-IV-B section of our own spacecraft, or possibly one or more of the four panels that peeled away when we extracted the lunar module (LM)—the vehicle in which Neil and I would land on the Moon—from our command and service vehicle. In moving the LM, the command vehicle in which Mike, Neil, and I were traveling was nose to nose with the LM for a while, and the four panels that had protected the LM fell away in four separate directions. With the Sun reflecting off one of the panels, still moving along with our spacecraft, it *seemed* as though a brightly lit object was following us. Which of the four panels? I don't know, so technically, there was an "unidentified flying object" in our rearview mirror.

After Neil, Mike, and I returned to Earth, we were debriefed by NASA scientists, and we mentioned the odd encounter with the unidentified flying object. NASA made little to-do about it, and we were thrilled with so many other aspects of the Apollo 11 mission that we had a lot of other things to talk about. We let the matter of the unidentified object drop.

A number of years later though, I was doing an interview with a foreign television network, and, assuming that NASA had made public our observations about the UFO, I told the story. When word got out that Apollo 11 astronauts had seen a UFO and not informed the world—especially those who adamantly believe in extraterrestrial presences in space—it caused a major uproar. In more places than I care to imagine, people were saying things such as, "Buzz saw an alien and NASA's covering it up and won't let him talk about it."

It *seemed* that way. But now you know what really happened.

As Carl Sagan was fond of noting about improbable possibilities, "Extraordinary claims require extraordinary evidence." Personally, I strongly believe other life-forms might exist in various places throughout the universe, but the tremendous distances involved in trying to explore the immenseness of the universe make discovery unlikely in the near future.

( 

DON'T LIVE YOUR LIFE BY what *seems* to be true. Other people may not "get" you. So what? It's not what you do or where you go, but who you are becoming that really matters. Although many people sit around worrying that a decision by a roomful of strangers is about to change their lives forever, the reality is that their lives have already been shaped decisively by the sum of their own past decisions—the habits developed, the friends made, and the challenges overcome. What you do or where you work or go to school matters, because those types of criteria often present a measure of the person you're becoming. But never allow other people to define your destiny. Who you work for and what you do are not nearly as important as who you *are*.

The important thing is that you believe in yourself and that you learn to maintain your composure, even under difficult circumstances. Handling pressure is a lifelong process, and the ability to remain calm or to regain self-control is key to thriving even in potentially frightening or life-threatening situations.

Why?

Because most people don't make their best decisions when they are angry or frightened or nervous. When your emotions are surging and running rampant, it is far too easy to make an irrational mistake, to do something really stupid that you may regret for a long time. Many of those emotion-driven, irrational responses could be avoided simply by taking time to breathe.

When somebody says something that angers you, rather than lashing back with equal venom, take a few moments (or hours, or days, if necessary) to calm down and make a more calculated response. Your actions will usually be wiser, better, and more effective when you have taken the emotional elements out of them as much as possible.

As fighter pilots, Neil and I learned the principle of not allowing our emotions to get the better of us in difficult circumstances. That training came in real handy on the Moon.

After completing our experiments on the lunar surface, Neil and I reentered the *Eagle,* and we threw out our "garbage" bag, containing anything that was contaminated, including the boots we wore on the lunar surface. I've always wished that we could have kept those boots.

When we completed our housecleaning chores, we repressurized the LM, putting oxygen back into the cabin, and depressurized our space suits. We snacked on cold cocktail sausages and fruit punch. After that, our checklist told us that it was time to sleep. On Earth, we had simulated being in and out of the LM many times, but we had never really determined how and where we were going to sleep while on the Moon. We had no beds or even cots in the lunar module. I took first dibs and decided to sleep on the floor, while Neil sat on the ascent engine cover and leaned back against a console with his feet off the ground.

It was cold in the cabin and hard to sleep in the cramped conditions. As I lay down and fidgeted on the floor, I turned my head and noticed some lunar dust we'd tracked in, but also something else—a piece of plastic that looked as though it had broken off something. It seemed like a circuit breaker, so I stood up and started looking over the row of circuit breakers, trying to determine where the plastic may have come from. My heart sank when I saw it.

To my dismay, the missing breaker was labeled **ENG ARM**, "Engine Arm," one of the most important switches in the *Eagle*. The checklist simply displayed a picture of the breakers: black = in; white = out. While we were stationary on the surface, it was perfectly safe for this breaker to be out, but the *Eagle* was designed so it is impossible to descend to the Moon with that circuit breaker pressed in, and it is impossible to get off the Moon with it popped out. This circuit was crucial to send the electrical current to light the ascent engine that would lift us off the Moon. Because the breaker was located on my side of the capsule, I had apparently bumped it with the heavy backpack either preparing to step outside or when we had come back inside after walking on the Moon.

As soon as I discovered the broken circuit breaker, we called Mission Control to inform them. We missed a golden opportunity to use the classic line immortalized by astronaut Jack Swigert a few years later, when he said, "Houston, we've had a problem here," as the crew encountered difficulties after an explosion on board Apollo 13, the mission commanded by Jim Lovell. Rather than landing on the Moon, the entire crew of Apollo 13 was forced to cram into the lunar landing module for the return flight home.

Although Neil and I didn't say it that way, we certainly did have a problem, but it wasn't ours alone; we figured it was Houston's problem, too, so they told us to go to sleep while they worked on a solution. They were hoping to somehow reroute the power to that absolutely essential circuit. Neil and I tried to get some sleep while the experts back on Earth debated what to do.

We checked in again six hours later. "Unfortunately," Mission Control informed us, "there is no way to reroute the power." The conclusion from the experts working on the problem in Houston was that we would have to push something in to activate the circuit.

We moved the time of pushing the breaker to two hours earlier on our flight schedule; we wanted to make sure the circuit would function while we still had some time to adapt. Houston said, "We'll just have to try it." If the circuit breaker didn't work, we could wait another two hours while Mike Collins orbited the Moon again, giving Mission Control more time to find a way to get us off the lunar surface. I wasn't really too worried about what might happen if the breaker didn't work. I chose to spend my time doing what we could do to fix the problem, and of course, Neil and I were relying on a great team of experts back on Earth.

I didn't want to push in the breaker with my pinky finger, or with a ballpoint pen, or anything metal—not with all that electrical power flowing into that circuit. But in our personal preference kits, I had included a plastic felt-tip pen. It wasn't on the official list of items we took to the Moon, but I now had that pen in the shoulder pocket of my space suit.

I gingerly pressed the pen against the engine arm circuit breaker. For a long moment, I didn't want to remove the tip from the circuit breaker, hoping against hope that it would hold. Slowly, almost reluctantly, I eased the pressure on my hand and lifted the pen's tip.

The pen did the trick; the circuit breaker held. We could return to Earth, after all!

( 

EVEN WITH ALL THE YEARS OF careful planning and training, something so small, like breaking the one circuit breaker that we needed to lift off the Moon to come home, could have derailed our plans. But with a little outside-the-box thinking and some simple improvisation, we were able to fix the problem, rendezvous with Mike, and return to Earth. Not panicking helps, too. That's why, all these years later, when people ask me what it "felt" like walking on the Moon, I usually answer, "Fighter pilots don't have feelings; we have ice water running in our veins."

When under pressure, you must remain focused on the immediate task in front of you, regardless of the distractions around you. Unfortunately, mistakes or accidents sometimes happen, even after the best preparation. To appropriately respond to an emergency requires a clear mind and the ability to analyze a situation and do what is necessary to fix it or make it better. Fear and worry will only cloud your mind and keep you from thinking clearly. Far better to have practiced procedures that you know will help you in the midst of a stressful situation. For instance, a fighter pilot doesn't want to dwell on the possibility of an engine failure as he is rolling down the runway. Instead, he is thinking about making a smooth takeoff. Nevertheless, in the back of his mind, he has rehearsed many times and he knows exactly what to do in case he has to hit the eject controls and leave that aircraft in a hurry!

In a similar manner, I learned as a child to look in both directions before crossing a street, and I still do so to this day. It is not fear that motivates me to check my surroundings but awareness that even the best laid plans can sometimes go awry.

In times of crisis, lead rather than follow. Establish yourself as an expert, the go-to person that others look to for insight or help. In other words, don't wait for someone to come to your rescue in life; figure out a way to do what you need to do. And don't merely be a strategist; at some point you need to become a *doer,* moving from deciding to doing. There's action, and then there's everything else.

To succeed in any environment, you have to believe in yourself. You must have an unshakable confidence in your own ability to achieve your goals and get the job done.

Trust yourself. Some of the worst mistakes of my life have occurred when I trusted other people to make important decisions for me. A key to success in any field is to take responsibility for your own actions. Always be open to advice from others, but what matters most is who you want to *be*, not merely what you want to do—and certainly not who or what others want you to be or do.

Figure out what makes *you* happy, content, well adjusted, no matter how crazy it may sound to other people. Determine what is important to you, what's in your heart and mind that you really believe, and then pursue that with all your might.

Master yourself—that's the toughest challenge you will ever have. Develop your disciplines ahead of time, so when the pressure is on, you just have to do it.

Oh, and perhaps most important: No excuses.

Unquestionably, all of the Apollo astronauts were selected for these missions because we had the right skills and emotional makeup for the job. But being able to adapt to situations was also critical to the success of our missions.

In subsequent Apollo launches, NASA placed a protective bar over the circuit breakers to prevent mishaps similar to ours. I still have that broken circuit breaker from Apollo 11 and the felt-tip pen that helped us get off the Moon. They are good reminders that when the pressure is on, you can't allow your emotions to overwhelm you; the best way to handle the situation is to maintain your composure.

Not that I've always done so perfectly—not by a long shot. One incident in which my composure was somewhat ruffled hit national news, made the rounds of the talk shows, and has been seen on YouTube more than five million times.

For years after I returned to Earth, my fellow astronauts and I were repeatedly accosted by conspiracy theory nuts claiming that the United States never really landed on the Moon, that the whole thing was done in a Hollywood-style studio, and that the landing was a hoax foisted on the public by the government. What lunacy! But there is no accounting for some people's logic, or lack of it.

I don't waste my time debating the obvious. Certainly, plenty of evidence is available to anyone who cares to examine it. Photographs from lunar reconnaissance orbiter satellites circling the Moon clearly show the *Eagle's* landing site and all of the experiments that Neil and I set up, and it is possible to view the path where Neil stirred up the dust by walking on the Moon to see the large crater that we had avoided. For any intelligent person, such recent photos should forever put an end to the conspiracy kooks claiming that we never landed on the Moon. Google has even posted a comparison between our original photos and video and a more recent attempt to reproduce our lunar landing, and the similarities are astounding.

Most of the conspiracy nuts are harmless—irritating, but nonetheless benign. One was not. He repeatedly harassed me with false accusations, impugning my character and claiming

I had never walked on the Moon. I could never figure out what he hoped to gain from his crazy assertions, other than trying to make a name for himself.

I had agreed to do an interview at a Beverly Hills hotel for what I thought was a Japanese children's program. But I quickly figured out the interview was a farce and that I had been tricked into showing up. As I tried to exit the hotel, my accoster repeatedly demanded that I swear on a Bible, which he brandished in my face, that I had walked on the Moon. I was offended for both the Bible and for me.

I was irritated by his incessant, rude, and irrelevant demands, but when he called me a coward and a liar and a thief . . . well, I could no longer maintain my composure. I punched the guy right in the jaw. The harasser's film crew recorded the entire incident, and he later tried to use the video to convince the police that I had assaulted him.

The video became a blessing in disguise because the police refused to entertain the charges, concluding that the accoster had repeatedly provoked me into decking him. Talk show hosts such as Jay Leno and David Letterman had a field day with the video clip, airing the incident on their shows. One show created a video spoof of Christopher Columbus being accosted by conspiracy nuts who claimed that he never discovered America. Of course, after putting up with the harassment for a few moments, Columbus decked the guy!

I'm glad to say that most people who have seen the video of my punch have sided with me, agreeing that my response was justified. It may not have been one of my most noble moments, but just as one picture is worth more than a thousand words . . .

As I said, you cannot always predict what will happen, no matter how well you have trained and prepared. Certainly, you can avoid many stressful situations simply by planning ahead as much as possible, but be prepared for the unexpected, too. Remember, even the best plans are not infallible. When things go wrong and you have to find a way to adapt, don't be afraid to change your plans. Just do what you have to do and make the best of a bad situation.

Because I travel by air quite often, I seek out airline hospitality lounges whenever I am awaiting a flight or experiencing delays. Often, even those airlines of which I am not a member of their "club" will invite me into their lounge as a professional courtesy. One time as I was awaiting a Delta Air Lines flight in Phoenix, Arizona, I approached the desk at the Delta lounge, and without mentioning my name, asked if I could enter.

"Are you a member, sir?" the receptionist asked. She smiled at me with one of those expressions that seems as though it is sealed in plastic.

"No, but I usually stop here when I'm flying through Phoenix," I said. "I just want to get a cup of coffee and make some calls."

"Well, sir, if you are not a member, you can purchase a one-day pass to our club today for forty dollars."

I knew the receptionist was simply doing her job, but I really didn't need to join another airline club. I peered at her intently, hoping that she might recognize me and change her mind.

She didn't. She gazed back at me with the same plastic expression.

I squinted at her even more intensely. Rarely do I say such things, but for some reason it seemed appropriate in this case. "Do you know who I am?" I asked, the folly of my question striking me the moment it left my lips.

"Oh, yes, Mr. Aldrin," she replied. "But if you want to come into our lounge, it will be forty dollars. Otherwise, there's a McDonald's right next door. You can get a cup of coffee there."

I nodded, thanked her, and went to McDonald's.

Sometimes, when God gives you lemons . . .

# CHAPTER ELEVEN

# LAUGH ... A LOT!

S tanding on E! Entertainment Television's set for the final episode of *Chelsea Lately,* along with numerous celebrities such as Jennifer Aniston, Gwen Stefani, Gerard Butler, Dave Grohl of the Foo Fighters, Melissa McCarthy, Sandra Bullock, and a host of others who had gathered together to sing a song for Chelsea's send-off, I was surrounded by Kathy Griffin, Joel McHale, and several others.

My Mission Control Director, Christina, said to me, "Buzz, these guys are comedians."

"Oh, really?" I asked. I looked at the group of professional comics around me and said, "Let me explain to you the meaning of humor, and what real humor involves."

The comedians gathered in closer, as if I were about to give them an insight they'd never heard before.

"You take a serious subject and you throw in an absurdity. And that's humor," I said.

The pros nodded appreciatively in agreement. Or at least I thought they were agreeing with me. Maybe they were merely humoring me.

To me, that's the way good humor works—add some absurdity into a common subject and then continue on as though everything is normal, and find the funny elements within it. Good humor need not be crass, profane, or offensive. Anyone can attempt to be funny by emphasizing vulgar elements of life or by going for shock value. But creative humor finds the funny in everyday life.

（

Nobody would consider me a comic, but even during Apollo 11, I attempted to find some levity in the midst of the tension.

For instance, we had no handle on the outside of the *Eagle*'s hatch, so as I was climbing out of the lunar module, with millions of people on Earth listening to Neil's and my every breath, I couldn't resist commenting. "Okay, now I want to back up and partially close the hatch," I said, "making sure not to lock it on my way out."

My statement was both factual and absurd at the same time, but I offered it without a chuckle, although my eyes were probably twinkling as brightly as the stars above me.

Already standing on the lunar surface, Neil Armstrong laughed out loud. "A particularly good thought," he responded.

We had discovered earlier that if the hatch was closed completely, the inside cabin pressure made it almost impossible to open, sealed by the external pressure on the Moon.

When Neil and I received word that we were good to take off from the lunar surface, I responded to our capsule communicator, Ron Evans, in Mission Control back in Houston, "Roger. Understand. We're number one on the runway."

My statement was comprised of two facts and two absurdities in the same sentence, so it was funny to me. It took the guys in Mission Control a few moments to catch my humor, and some never did!

(

LIFE IS SERIOUS, BUT don't take yourself so seriously. Be willing to make light of yourself. And here's a corollary to my theory of humor: Humor at the expense of others isn't nearly as funny as making light of yourself. I take my work and my ideas very seriously, but I'm quick to laugh at myself, even making fun of some of my personal indiscretions and mistakes in life.

When I received an invitation to appear as myself on the NBC sitcom *30 Rock,* I was intrigued. After all, *30 Rock* is an abbreviation for the building located at 30 Rockefeller Plaza in New York City, which is now home to the NBC television network, but as I was growing up, it was home to Standard Oil of New Jersey, where my father worked as an aviation fuel manager. So when I was asked to join Tina Fey and the cast of *30 Rock,* I jumped at the chance.

In the episode, Liz Lemon (Tina's character) laments that she will never find a man like her mother's great love, Eddie. We actually satirized some of the negative details from my own life experiences to help Liz realize that the ideal astronaut does not exist. Ironically, I was telling her the truth! These were some of my failures and low points; they were not my best qualities. But I was glad we could laugh about them—in the fictional scene as well as in real life.

The way the story was set up, Liz's mother had been telling her stories for years about her ideal man: Eddie the Astronaut. Meanwhile, Liz had been holding out for her ideal man, Mike Dexter. But then she meets me and realizes the truth.

Liz enters a glass-surrounded penthouse room and finds me looking out the windows at New York. "Excuse me, Doctor Aldrin," she says. "I'm sorry, there wasn't a door, so I just . . ."

"I don't believe in barriers, because I always break them. You must be Liz!"

"Yes, sir." Liz crosses the room and faces me. "I actually came about my mother, Margaret Lemon. You would have known her as Margaret Freeman?"

"Maggie Freeman. Of course, I remember her."

"Well, I'm sorry to bother you, but I can't help but wonder what my mom lost by giving up on you, her perfect man."

"Perfect? Sure, I'm a famous astronaut, decorated fighter pilot, doctorate through MIT, but even I sometimes . . ." Distracted, I break off in mid-sentence, go to the windows, and address the Moon in the sky. "I see you! I see what you're doing. Return to the night! You've no business here."

"Are you yelling at the Moon?" Liz asks.

"I'm sorry . . . she and I just . . . I get mad sometimes."

"Sure . . ."

"Look, do you want to know what your mother missed? Years of drinking, depression, cheating. I flipped over a Saab in the San Fernando Valley. I once woke up in the Air and Space Museum with a revolver in the waistband of my jean shorts!"

"Oh, my god, but you were a . . ."

"A human being," I interrupt Liz, "but I'm at peace now, sober almost 32 years. But I would have put Maggie Freeman through hell."

Liz sighs in frustration.

"There's no such thing as astronaut Mike Dexter. What am I doing?"

"I'm sorry if I've disappointed you," I say to Liz. "Would you like to yell at the Moon with Buzz Aldrin?"

"Yes! Please."

Liz and I go to the large windows facing the cityscape and raise our faces toward the Moon, even though it's broad daylight.

"I own you!" I yell at the Moon.

"You dumb Moon!" Liz agrees, shaking her fist at the Moon.

"I walked on your face!"

"Don't you know it's day? Idiot!" Liz adds.

I loved working with Tina Fey. She is bright, talented, and so much fun. And she is cute, too. When Tina was asked to contribute a photo for a book about New York, choosing something that was iconically New York, she included a photo of the two of us on the set of *30 Rock*. It was definitely one of my favorite sitcoms on which I appeared.

(

I ALWAYS ENJOY spoofing myself. I made a cameo appearance on the CBS television hit *The Big Bang Theory,* a show that finds humor in the lives of a group of astrophysicists, engineers, and physicists. In the episode, Raj wants to pop Howard's balloon a bit and bring him back to Earth, since he has become obnoxiously boastful about traveling into space as an astronaut. Besides wearing a NASA shirt every day and passing out eight-by-ten glossies of himself in uniform, Howard has developed an annoying habit of turning every conversation toward space. I cannot imagine why they wanted *me* in this segment!

Howard's wife, Bernadette, confronts him about his bloviating, but rather than accepting the critique graciously, Howard becomes defensive, disappointed that his wife and friends are dumping on his great achievements. Raj sends a video link to Howard, ostensibly featuring me passing out trick-or-treat candy to kids coming to my door. The role had me boasting about my accomplishments as an astronaut every time I handed out a piece of Halloween candy, somehow connecting each treat to my experiences in space.

I hand the first little boy a Milky Way candy bar as I explain, "There you go; it's a Milky Way. The Milky Way is a galaxy in space." I point at my chest and say, "I've been in space."

To a little girl, I say, "It's a Mars bar," as I give her the candy. "I'm an astronaut."

When the third child approaches, a slightly older boy dressed as a fireman, I hand him a MoonPie and say, "This one's a MoonPie! I've walked on the Moon." I hold my hands out as though begging for an answer and ask, "What have you done with your life?"

After the third over-the-top trick-or-treat exchange, Howard sheepishly turns to Bernadette and admits, "Okay, I get it."

E! Entertainment Television declared my cameo as "one of the funniest, yet shortest, guest spots in *BBT* history."

My role on the show wasn't completely accurate. Contrary to bragging about landing on the Moon, I've always been quite conscious of the fact that I was simply the right guy in the right place at the right time. I've always felt fortunate to have had the tremendous opportunity afforded me—lucky to have been born an American, lucky to have been selected as an astronaut, and lucky to have been part of the initial crew to land on another celestial body. Of course, the humorous point was not lost on me that I can easily become too verbose when talking about space. Howard, I get it, too!

( 

EVEN WHEN I'M NOT on television, I occasionally come up with a zinger. For instance, one time Christina and I had just landed at the airport, coming home from Germany, when a reporter from TMZ asked me, "What did you think of that Felix Baumgartner leaping off the Red Bull hot-air balloon today?"

It was quite an impressive feat, as Baumgartner jumped from 24 miles high, an altitude of more than 100,000 feet, and reached airspeeds as high as 500 miles an hour, whisking downward, wearing only a space suit and helmet for protection and relying on a parachute to slow his fall once he reached 10,000 feet. Responding instinctively, I said, "That was one giant leap for Red Bull." To me, that was a zinger, taking a serious subject and throwing in an absurdity.

Sometimes you just have to roll with it.

During a 2015 congressional hearing on America's future in space, chaired by Texas senator Ted Cruz, I was giving a presentation, waxing quite eloquently on the potential of exploration, when I was interrupted by a cell phone ringing. I reached into my pocket and realized that the ringing cell phone was mine! I pulled out the phone and said, "Sorry," as I turned off the phone.

Senator Cruz had a quick response. "Please tell us that is not a call from the space station." We all had a laugh at my expense, and I carried on with my presentation. I'm usually a pretty good sport, even going on *Sesame Street* once to explain that the Moon is not made of cookie dough, so appearing at a Senate subcommittee hearing was a piece of cake!

How you respond to what life throws at you often makes all the difference. Smile. Laugh. Don't take yourself so seriously. When *you* change, everything else around you changes.

Everywhere I travel, people tell me stories of where they were that day in 1969 when Neil and I walked on the Moon.

They tell me about the incredible celebrations and parties in which they participated in honor of Apollo 11, and I get envious. I would have loved to have attended some of those parties, but Neil, Mike, and I were out of town!

Hey, that's pretty funny!

And you thought astronauts were dull!

# CHAPTER TWELVE

# KEEP A YOUNG MIND-SET AT EVERY AGE.

Y ou may get older chronologically, but you don't have to grow an old-person mentality. Instead, maintain a youthful outlook—regardless of your age. Count your blessings, and enjoy every moment of life.

We all know that getting old is not for sissies. Sure, there are some things I just cannot do, or shouldn't do, in my mid-80s that I did in my mid-20s. I'm getting older, but I don't see myself as an old person, and I don't think "old." Instead, whenever someone asks me my age, I prefer to say, "I am 86 going on 40!"

One of the keys to having a young attitude is to surround yourself with younger people. I like having bright, ambitious, motivated young people around me. I enjoy their enthusiasm, and I am energized by their spirit. I embrace their technology rather than complaining that I cannot get the LED light to stop blinking on an appliance in my home.

Sure, there are times when I don't act my age. Not long ago, Christina and I were having a disagreement. I was complaining about something and Christina responded, "Oh, Buzz, quit being a big baby."

"I'm not a big baby," I retorted. "I'm an old fart!"

"Okay, fine; quit being an old fart who is acting like a big baby," Christina replied. Her response lightened the mood and we both broke out laughing.

Clearly, adulthood and maturity do not necessarily come with age. You can grow old but never grow up; growing older does not guarantee growing in maturity. You need someone around you who is honest and who cares enough to look you in the eye and say, "Straighten up! You're not flying right."

For years, that person in my life was my older sister, Fay Ann. She called me almost every day, and she held me accountable and seemed to know the right thing to say to me. She was always an encourager. Not that she was always easy on me—quite the contrary; she'd call things the way she saw them.

One day I was complaining to Fay Ann about pain in my elbow.

"What's wrong with your elbow?" my sister asked.

"Oh, I'm really unhappy. I had surgery and I don't think it was done right. I think this surgery was a failure. My arm still hurts."

"When did you have the surgery?" Fay Ann probed.

"Yesterday," I said.

Fay Ann was exasperated at my lack of patience. "At our age, healing takes a little longer," she said. "Sure, we're going to have some health problems, but we have to accept who we are, wherever we are in life. And we also have to take care of ourselves. So suck it up, little brother."

Since Fay Ann passed away in 2012, and my other sister, Maddy, passed away in 2015, Christina is now my conscience and my indispensable crutch. Like my mother and my sisters, she is not a "yes person," so she, too, holds me accountable, and I will be forever grateful.

Strong women have helped shape who I am—especially my mom and my two sisters, as well as my daughter, Jan. Consequently, I've never looked down on women or felt they were inferior to men or not as intelligent as me. And when I meet a bright woman, I love being able to communicate with her about things that really matter. My sisters, Fay Ann and Maddy, might have made great astronauts, but unfortunately, that was not an option for them during the period of time in which they lived. They were very smart, and at one point were doing way better academically than I was. My parents pointed this out to me and said, "If you don't watch it, your sisters are going to leave you in the dust!" That certainly got my attention and helped me to focus on my studies. Later on, my sisters did what young women of that time were expected to do. They got married and had children, and although they enjoyed their lives, I wonder what they might have done if given the opportunities I had received.

The good news is that times have changed; a world of opportunities now exists for both men and women, and women need not be trapped by the stereotypes of the past. Women are now able to do anything men can do in the space program, and I'm confident we will see more women going into space in the years to come.

(

NOWADAYS, I MOVE A BIT MORE slowly, and I am more careful than when I was a young man. I have enough physical maladies, so I am careful when I go up and down stairs, because I've heard of older people falling and incurring disabling injuries. I don't want that to happen. But regardless of your age, you have to take time to dip your toes in the water. I see lots of people lying out on the beach getting suntans, or others walking up and down the beach, but very few getting into the water. Not me. I like to get my feet wet!

We have to accept where we are in life, and every age can be exciting if you continue to pursue new adventures. Don't allow yourself to grow stale, to stagnate due to health problems, financial issues, lack of stimulation, or anything else.

How do you measure your life? What moments have changed your life . . . or will change your life? Are you living or existing?

Oh, sure, I've come close to dying a few times, but usually I was having so much fun at the time that I barely noticed the danger. For instance, on one occasion, I was scuba diving in Malta with some friends. Around 120 feet down, I noticed an enormous school of tropical fish. Oddly, they were all moving in a clockwise direction, making huge circles. I wanted to take a closer look, so I dove deeper to check them out. I swam right into the huge school of fish, and let the fish swim straight at me as I looked them right in the eyes.

I glanced down and noticed a dive photographer below me taking pictures. About that time, my dive computer's emergency notice sounded, beep, beep, *beep!* I had become so mesmerized by the unusual school of fish and was having so much fun that I had neglected to pay attention to my depth. I was too deep, coming up too quickly, and I was in danger of decompression. About that time, my dive computer indicated SOS and shut off completely!

The real problem in a situation such as this was that nitrogen had gotten into my bloodstream at much higher pressure while I was deep underwater. Ordinarily, that's not too serious if a diver comes up slowly, taking regular decompression stops along the way, but if you ascend too quickly, air embolism occurs and your lungs cannot handle it. The nitrogen bubbles in your bloodstream don't dissipate. Instead, they respond much like a bottle of soda that is shaken up and then suddenly opened. The gas is released and enlarged bubbles cause whatever is in the can or bottle to come bursting out. Now imagine that happening to your lungs and blood vessels. That is known as the bends, a very dangerous condition that can be extremely painful in your knee joints, and can even be fatal because of rupturing veins and all sorts of other associated problems.

This was one of the few times that I was really nervous about the possibility of dying. *I might not make it out of this one,* I thought. I was fortunate that I made it back to the surface and my body slowly readjusted. I felt okay, so I didn't mention my close call to anyone—until now.

(

WE'RE ALL GOING TO DIE. There's no question about that. The real question is whether or not you have lived.

Sure, I have health issues just as most other people in their 80s, but I get up every morning, arrange all the pills and vitamins I have to take, pour a cup of coffee, and enjoy my breakfast as I read the newspaper. It is a new day, filled with opportunities. Why should I focus on what I can no longer do when there are so many things I still can and want to enjoy?

I hear some people complaining about growing older. Why would I want to do that? After all, think of the other options! I'm not ashamed of my age; in fact, I revel in my years. I've enjoyed a wonderful life, and I'm going to keep on living it to the fullest for as long as I can! I get up every morning looking forward to the future, because there's still a lot of work for me to do.

Here in a nutshell are some more simple lessons I've learned over the past 86 years: Look for the good, and you will find it. Accept the bitter with the sweet, and be happy in both. Truth is, the bitter may be better for us in the long run because we probably grow and learn more from the bitter things we've experienced in life than we do from the sweet things. Regardless, stay positive in your attitude, and don't carry around a bunch of negative thoughts and feelings. They won't do you any good, and they won't be of help to anyone else. Don't waste your time—we only have so much of it, yet we often don't realize that until it is too late. Don't fritter away your future by dwelling on some failure from the past. If you fall down, brush yourself off, get up, and keep looking forward. Take care of your body; it's the only one you get so make sure you nourish it with healthy food and restful sleep. I've never pampered my body, but I've also been careful not to mistreat it, and that has been a good balance for me over the years.

( 

I'VE DONE A FEW THINGS THAT have taxed my endurance. Surprisingly, one of those was appearing on the 2010 season of the television show *Dancing With the Stars*.

Christina called me while I was in a meeting in Washington, D.C., trying to explain my unified space vision and my Mars Cycler to the science adviser to the president and several other White House staff people. Ordinarily, I wouldn't take a phone call in the middle of a meeting, but I noticed that it was Christina calling, and because she knew I was in a meeting at the White House, I assumed it must be important.

"The casting director for the television show *Dancing With the Stars* wants you to be on the program next season," she said. "Would you want to do *Dancing With the Stars?*"

"Okay. Yeah, sure, I'll do that." I was just trying to get Christina off the phone, so I could get back to my meeting.

"Do you know what that is?"

"No," I said, "but that's okay. I'll do it."

"It's a television show where celebrities dance with professionals and they teach you how to do ballroom dances."

"Okay," I said again, trying to hang up as quickly as possible.

Christina was surprised. She hadn't really expected me to say yes, so she reiterated the details of the invitation. "You have to dance."

"Okay, I can do that."

"It's a lot of work, Buzz," Christina cautioned. "They rehearse six to eight hours a day all week long."

"Okay, sure. Fine," I answered, barely hearing Christina's warning. "I can do that."

"Okay . . ." She booked me on the show.

I had recently been in the recording studio with legendary music producer Quincy Jones, doing a rap song about rockets with Snoop Dogg, so I felt confident that I had some sense of rhythm and could be rather fluid on the dance floor and that I could do whatever dances were required on the show.

After all, I had learned to dance as a young man, taking lessons at the Arthur Murray Dance Studio, and we had been required to learn formal ballroom-style dances at West Point. I had also occasionally attended West Point dances called "hops." Beyond that, on the world tour following the Apollo 11 mission, I had danced at a number of formal balls and had danced with "Miss Kinshasa," the local beauty queen in the Democratic Republic of the Congo, after having sat outside in triple-digit temperatures as Neil, Mike, and I listened respectfully to the national anthems of seven different countries. No wonder when I came down off the platform and danced with Miss Kinshasa, her body odor nearly knocked me over. I may have held my nose, but I danced!

Neil later upbraided me for making a spectacle of myself by stepping off the platform to dance with the local beauty queen. The unflappable Apollo 11 commander might have really flipped had he known that I had spent a night dancing with Italian bombshell actress Gina Lollobrigida a few months later on our tour.

I like beautiful women and I like to dance with them, so why not go on *Dancing With the Stars*? What could be so difficult about that? Boy, was I ever in for a surprise!

The cast included blond bombshell Pamela Anderson, known around the world from her stint on *Baywatch;* Nicole Scherzinger of Pussycat Dolls' fame; Kate Gosselin, a reality show star; sports broadcaster Erin Andrews; NFL football player Chad "Ochocinco" Johnson; TV "Bachelor" Jake Pavelka; actors Aiden Turner and Niecy Nash; and Olympic gold medalist skater Evan Lysacek.

I had actually met Evan earlier and presented him with an Omega wristwatch when he won a gold medal at the Vancouver Winter Olympics. At the time, neither of us could have guessed that we'd be ballroom dancing on a television show in front of millions of viewers.

When we gathered for the initial photo shoot and the announcement of the new cast members, the producers asked me to wear a military uniform, which I was honored to do. To complete the look, I wore my genuine Medal of Freedom that had been presented to me by the president of the United States. Evan, the Olympic champion, brought his gold medal, so we stood together for photos showing off our medals—Evan's for skating, and mine for . . . well, you know.

Practicing for *Dancing With the Stars* was almost as tough as astronaut workouts. I honestly think it was the most difficult exercise regimen I've ever experienced. Maybe it was my age, but the *Dancing With the Stars* rehearsals may even have been more strenuous than my West Point conditioning, in which a part of cadets' training included running up and down stairs while carrying 50-pound sacks on our shoulders.

My professional dance partner was Ashly Costa, a gorgeous, dark-eyed, dark-haired beauty. When I first met Ashly, I thought, *This is a really cute babe!* And as she taught me the dance steps, I had no problem keeping my eyes on her! Following her instructions? Now, that was another matter.

We rehearsed at a dance studio in Hollywood all day long, from early morning till late afternoon, every day for several weeks prior to the first show. It was challenging, but I loved being around all the attractive young people, and I seemed to draw energy from them, feeling younger and more vigorous myself. They all treated me with tremendous respect, and of course, I explained to them how they could one day be dancing on Mars.

Those kids are really in great physical shape. I was not. But thanks to the strenuous rehearsals, I actually lost a good bit of weight during the run-up to my "live" performances on the show.

One day while we were rehearsing for a group number, it was rather warm, so some of the young guys took off their shirts and rehearsed wearing only their sweatpants. Nodding toward the washboard stomachs of a couple of the male dancers, I said, "I used to look like that." At one of the next rehearsals, I brought in a photo taken of me in a swimsuit, when I had been scuba diving and was young and buff. "See, I told you, I used to look like you guys," I quipped.

The young professional dancers were wonderfully complimentary. "You still look like that, Buzz!" Russian-born Maks Chmerkovskiy said. Maks and Derek Hough were tremendously encouraging to me during my time on the show.

All the girls were great to me, too. I loved dancing with the beautiful girls on the show, and simply hanging out with the young people was invigorating for me.

Ashly encouraged me to turn off my mind and move to the music. That was especially difficult for me, because I was not accustomed to *not* thinking about what I was trying to do. I was having a bit of trouble figuring out the steps, so I told Ashly that I needed to sketch out "the trajectories" for where I needed to go on the dance floor during the numbers on which I would be dancing. I plotted out the dance trajectories so I would know where to go and what I needed to do. Once I got the dance thing down in rendezvous concepts that I could understand, I was okay!

Our first dance on the show's season premiere was a cha-cha to the Sam Cooke version of "Cupid," a dance with a lot of quick movements. Ashly tried to come up with choreography that worked well for me but still covered the dance floor and played up to the audience and the judges. For our performance, Ashly wore a sparkling red dress, and I wore a bright red shirt with a dazzling black vest covered in diamond-like rhinestones.

The dance went as well as could be expected, and the crowd applauded enthusiastically. One of the studio audience members seen applauding during the telecast was actor Tim Allen, the voice of Buzz Lightyear.

Ashly and I thought the routine went well, but the judges didn't agree. The cranky, "older" judge, Len Goodman, began his critique of our routine by complimenting me. "I remember sitting at home in England watching you walking on the Moon and being amazed," Len said, "not only at the technology, but the braveness of you guys for going up there for the first time."

"Very lucky guys," I agreed.

Then Len, a longtime professional ballroom dancer, declared his opinion of my dancing ability. "I want to commend you for your bravery coming out tonight. Unfortunately, I cannot give marks for bravery, just the dancing, and that wasn't too good."

The studio audience of more than 700 people howled in disapproval.

The quick-witted Tom Bergeron, the show's host, jumped in and asked Len, "And how is that British space program going?" Len just shook his head and laughed.

Bruno Tonioli began by asking, "How can I criticize a hero and a legend?" But of course he did. "It's my job," he said.

Bruno told me, "You did a cha-cha-cha . . . but it looked like you had your Moon boots on." Then, apparently trying to find something positive, Bruno said, "Let's say it is going to get better next week."

The third judge, Carrie Ann Inaba, picked up on one of my main reasons for doing the show in the first place. "You know, what is great about this show is that it inspires people at home to get out and do things they might be afraid of."

"That's right," I agreed.

"You sure inspired a ton of people tonight," Carrie Ann complimented me. I appreciated the judges' kind words, but they still awarded Ashly and me the lowest scores of the evening.

The following week, for the fox-trot, I danced to the classic Frank Sinatra song "Fly Me to the Moon." Wearing a tuxedo and a sparkling silver bow tie, I began the dance by saluting the American flag and ended it in front of an American flag, reminiscent of the one Neil and I planted on the Moon 41 years previously.

Once again, although our routine was a hit with the audience — they gave us a long, enthusiastic standing ovation — the judges were unimpressed. "The man on the Moon looks stuck on the fox-trot," Bruno commented. "You look like you were avoiding craters," he added.

Ashly and I performed the waltz to "What a Wonderful World." For this dance, I was dressed in a striking military uniform, replete with my silver bow tie, attire to which I was accustomed. In the dancing story line and scenario, Ashly was supposed to be my daughter who was meeting me as I came home at the end of the war. To me, it was a story of patriotism and optimism about our future. At some point in the choreography, I was supposed to take off my hat and throw it. But in the excitement of the moment out on the dance floor with Ashly, I forgot to remove the hat. In the middle of the dance, I thought, *Uh-oh, I still have the hat on. How can I get rid of the hat without messing up my motions?* I kept the hat on all the way through the routine, but when one of the judges said something disparaging about my dancing talent, I took the hat off and threw it at him!

Naturally, some people said my performance was wooden and stiff, but the audience was wonderfully gracious, giving Ashly and me another prolonged standing ovation following our waltz. Ashly truly brought such grace to the dance, and I tried my best to reciprocate with charm.

Although I was the oldest person on the show at 80 years of age, the show staff didn't excuse me from any rehearsals or rigorous practice sessions. At one point during rehearsals, I had an already scheduled space conference and speaking engagement in New Zealand. *Dancing With the Stars* sent Ashly along with me on the trip so we could continue practicing our dances, even though we were halfway around the world. Ashly was a trooper and never once complained about the long way to work. I filmed Ashly on my phone so I could review the steps she was teaching me, even at home.

For two weeks in a row, Ashly and I landed at the bottom of the leaderboard with the lowest scores of all the dancers. But we still received tremendous support from fans of the show. Nevertheless, we were the second couple voted out of the competition, and the fact that I was "second" once again did not go unnoticed by pundits. I didn't mind. At least I was consistent! Besides, I'd been having the time of my life.

"I never thought I'd walk on the Moon, but I certainly never thought I'd dance on TV," I told host Tom Bergeron on camera after learning that Ashly and I had been voted off the competition. "I did this show for the fighter pilots out there, the military people, and the elder geezers like me who would just like to see an elder come back week after week," I added. I could feel a tear forming in my eye, so I hastily concluded my remarks, "It's been a wonderful experience for me."

For the season finale, although I had been eliminated, the producers asked Ashly and me to return and do a special dance along with other contestants and professionals who had been voted off the show. For our portion of the routine, the band played the *Star Wars* theme song. I was dressed in an aluminum-colored, "diamond"-studded spaceflight suit and shimmering silver cape and was surrounded by streams of green laser lights. I removed the cape and flipped it over to reveal a bright blue fabric, which I then wrapped around Ashly's waist. Near the end of the number, I removed the wrap from Ashly and held it out in bullfighter fashion as she did one final swirling movement and slid gracefully onto the floor in front of me as I held the cape above her. It was great fun, and the audience loved it.

The competition was intense, and Nicole Scherzinger won the famed mirror ball trophy. Evan Lysacek earned second place on the show.

When people ask me why I did the show, I repeat the three reasons I mentioned to Bergeron: to inspire interest in the space program, to honor veterans, and with hopes of motivating some other "elder geezers" like me to see that life isn't over just because we get a little older.

(

A FEW MONTHS LATER, I was performing in a cameo part for the movie *Transformers 3,* directed by the talented Michael Bay. I ripped through my lines and hit all my spots, without breaking a sweat.

Sitting in an area behind the monitor, Bay was watching like a mesmerized little kid, with his face in his hands. Michael whispered to Christina, "Does Buzz *ever* get nervous?"

"Only on *Dancing With the Stars,*" Christina answered.

(

I STILL DO A LITTLE DANCING once in a while. John Travolta helped me host a 2015 gala at the Kennedy Space Center for ShareSpace, my foundation dedicated to promoting science literacy among children. The moment John showed up, he automatically took the pressure off me and I knew I could relax. Not because I thought that he might not come, but because I knew that everybody would want to talk with John. He was a trooper and was glad to help lift the load off my shoulders.

Near the end of the gala, somebody suggested that we could boost the donations to ShareSpace if John Travolta and I got up and danced together. I was reluctant, but John insisted.

"Come on, Buzz. I'll show you a couple of moves."

John and I go way back, having first met on the set of the made-for-television movie *The Boy in the Plastic Bubble,* in which John starred and I had a bit part. The movie was hugely successful, garnering more than 45 million viewers. John is also a pilot, so we have aviation in common as well.

When we got out there in front of the crowd, I was afraid John would start into some of the moves he made famous in the movie *Saturday Night Fever,* with his head cocked to one side, his legs spread wide as though he were straddling a bull, and his hand high in the air. Fortunately for me, he did a much simpler routine. I did my best to copy him, but my body wouldn't move as well as his. We had great fun, though, and raised a bunch of money to help young people learn more about space exploration.

More and more these days, I feel my own mortality. I recognize that I'm getting older; I know that every day is a gift, and something could hit me at any time. I had a stroke in Vienna years ago, and it was a frightening experience. I worry sometimes that I don't have enough time left.

I've never been an overtly religious person, but I certainly understand those who are, and I have the greatest respect for them.

Long before I squeezed inside the command module of Apollo 11, perched on top of the huge Saturn V rocket that would send us racing toward the Moon, I realized that our mission would be fraught with symbolism. That's one of the reasons why Neil, Mike, and I chose as our mission emblem an eagle carrying an olive branch, signifying our hopes that peace on Earth could somehow be enhanced because of our landing on the Moon.

Once we had landed safely on the Moon, our schedule included time to eat a meal and to rest. As a gesture of my thankfulness, I planned to participate in a personal spiritual experience by celebrating Holy Communion as one of my first actions on the lunar surface.

The idea wasn't original to me. Explorers such as Christopher Columbus and other pioneers had done similar things when they had first landed in their new worlds. So a few weeks before our launch date, I asked my friend and pastor Dean Woodruff, minister at Webster Presbyterian Church where I attended when I was home in Houston, to help me. Dean provided some Communion wafers and a tiny chalice that I could take with me to the Moon.

Originally, I had thought of doing something more dramatic, celebrating on behalf of the entire world. But NASA had received flak following the Apollo 8 mission when astronauts Bill Anders, Jim Lovell, and Frank Borman had read from the Bible as they orbited the Moon on Christmas Eve.

Millions of people watched and listened as lunar module pilot Bill Anders spoke from space, "We are now approaching lunar sunrise, and for all the people back on Earth, the crew of Apollo 8 has a message that we would like to send to you." Anders then began reading the Genesis account of creation as recorded in the King James Version of the Bible: "In the beginning God created the heaven and the earth . . ."

The command module pilot, Jim Lovell, picked up the reading from there: "And God called the firmament Heaven . . . "

Apollo 8's commander, Frank Borman, concluded the reading: "And God said, 'Let the waters under the heavens be gathered together into one place, and let the dry land appear': and it was so. And God called the dry land Earth, and the gathering together of the waters called he Seas: and God saw that it was good."

Frank then added, "And from the crew of Apollo 8, we close with good night, good luck, a Merry Christmas, and may God bless all of you—all of you on the good Earth."

People of every religion—as well as most people who held to no religion—found the astronauts' readings inspiring. But atheist Madalyn Murray O'Hair filed a lawsuit against NASA, claiming that astronauts worked for the government, so their actions and words were a violation of the separation of church and state. The court eventually tossed out the case, but NASA didn't want any similar hassles.

So a few weeks prior to launch, when I told Deke Slayton, one of the original NASA astronauts who now ran the Apollo 11 flight crew operations, what I planned to do, Deke balked. "No, that's not a good idea, Buzz," he cautioned me. "Go ahead and have Communion, but keep your comments more general."

I didn't agree with Deke at the time, but I understood and complied with his instructions. Looking back, he was probably right.

Once Neil and I had shut down the engines and completed our checklist, from my position in the *Eagle,* now located on the Sea of Tranquility, I radioed Mission Control. "I would like to request a few moments of silence," I said, "and invite each person listening in, wherever and whomever they may be, to pause for a moment and contemplate the events of the past few hours, and to give thanks in his or her own way."

My way was with a symbolic wafer and thimbleful of wine that I had packed in my personal belongings pouch. We had little room for extras on board the *Eagle,* but the Communion elements didn't take up much space, and this was something special that I wanted to do, not just for myself but as a symbolic act of gratefulness for all mankind.

I pulled out a three-by-five card on which I had written the words of Jesus: "I am the vine, you are the branches. Whoever remains in me, and I in him, will bear much fruit; for you can do nothing without me." During the few moments of silence, I read the words on the card quietly, to myself. Then I pulled out the Communion wafer and the sealed plastic container of wine and poured it into the chalice Dean had given to me from our church. Although it was a spiritual moment, I was still a scientist, so I couldn't help noticing that in the Moon's gravity—only one-sixth of that on Earth—the wine curled ever so slowly and gracefully up the side of the chalice before finally settling after a few moments. I slipped the wafer into my mouth and then drank the wine. I didn't tell anyone what I was doing, and Neil looked on respectfully and silently as well. I offered a silent prayer of thanks and for the work yet to be done. Neither NASA nor anyone else in the U.S. government ever let on what I had done during the moments of silence on the Moon.

Over the years, I've often wondered if I did the right thing, that perhaps I should not have engaged in such an overtly Christian rite, because we wanted to emphasize that we had traveled to the Moon on behalf of all mankind—Christians, Jews, Muslims, Hindus, agnostics, and even atheists. But I cannot deny history. The truth is: The first liquid ever poured and the first food ever eaten on the Moon were Christian Communion elements.

At the time, I could think of no better way to acknowledge the enormous achievement of Apollo 11 than by giving thanks to God. When I got back home, I returned the small chalice to Webster Presbyterian Church. The church treated it as a special part of its history, encased it in a glass ball, and displayed it in the church library for all to see. Then oddly, for a time, the chalice mysteriously went missing. Years later, the church received a box in the mail. Inside was the chalice and a typed note of explanation. The sender admitted to taking the chalice as a youngster, not really understanding the significance of it or the seriousness of stealing it. Now, as an adult, the person realized that the chalice belonged to the church—and to the world. It was returned, and the congregation continues to celebrate a special Lunar Communion every year. Today, however, they display a replica chalice, and the original is now in a safety deposit box.

Symbols matter, and my hope was—and is—that people of any faith can celebrate the goodness of God and the achievements of mankind. Regardless of how you believe the universe was created, it is there waiting for humans to explore.

Recently, Christina and I were talking about religious subjects and I surprised her by saying, "I think I may be an atheist."

"I don't think you're an atheist," Christina countered.

"You don't? Why not? I'm certainly a skeptic."

"Yes, but you also believe in a higher power."

She had a good point. I'd seen numerous men and women find real strength and hope to overcome the strongest addictions by looking to a higher power. On the other hand, I've been all over the world, I've met people who hold to all sorts of religions, and I have encountered many diverse cultures. I've met good people in all walks of life. That has given me a different perspective on my faith. Who am I to criticize or demean anyone else's religious beliefs?

I don't go around giving testimony to my faith, and when anyone asks me about the Communion on the Moon, I tell them that I wanted to do something that was symbolic and something that was appropriate for the magnitude of what we had accomplished. The best way to do that was to encourage everyone to give thanks in their own way.

I am not afraid of dying, but what concerns me is that I might run out of time before I get everything done that I want to do. And there is so much more that I want to do! There are so many things I want to accomplish and people I want to impact. I'm not done yet. I have more to contribute. As a matter of fact, keep your eye on me; you ain't seen nuthin' yet!

SOMETIMES, THOUGH, THE LITTLE irritants in life create discomfort and distress. That's why you need to learn to deal with them quickly, rather than allowing them to continue to bug you.

Several astronauts, including Gene Cernan, Tom Stafford, and I were invited to attend the 2012 Olympics held in London. Everyone was excited because the phenomenal U.S. swimmer Michael Phelps would be attempting to win unprecedented 16th, 17th, and 18th gold medals.

We were in a hurry, so I had to get dressed quickly, and as we piled into the van that would take us to the swimming pool arena, I noticed a pain in my foot. "Gosh, my foot is killing me," I said to Christina.

"Are you sure you want to go?" she asked. "We can stay at the hotel."

"No, no," I downplayed the pain. "I'm all right."

When we arrived at the Olympic area, our van driver dropped us off as close as possible, but we still had to walk quite a distance to get to the VIP lounge that Olympic officials had so generously provided for us. As we walked, I felt the discomfort in my foot getting worse, and said so to Christina.

"Well, stop for a second and check. Is there something in your shoe?" Christina asked.

"No, no, let's keep going."

When we arrived in the reception room, I temporarily forgot about the pain in my foot as Gene Cernan and I got caught up in a conversation about our "fighter pilots' vision." Over the years, my eye doctors had occasionally recommended

I wear glasses to improve my vision. Instead, I had undergone four surgeries and other medical procedures to help my eyes overcorrect and counteract the normal effects of aging. As Gene and I were talking about it, Christina interjected, "I just don't understand why you don't simply wear glasses."

Gene jumped in, "Oh, no, no! You don't understand. We're fighter pilots. We've had perfect vision for most of our lives. We don't want to wear glasses now. I'm with Buzz on this one."

I smiled. Gene and I had known each other since working on the Gemini and Apollo space programs, and I think this was the first time he and I had ever agreed on anything! Christina knew it was futile to further discuss any corrective lenses for either of us.

Soon it was time for us to leave the VIP lounge and head for our seats at the swimming competition. We watched several preliminary heats, and Michael Phelps won two more gold medals, and I still had the pain in my foot! Finally, after nearly four hours since I first noticed the discomfort, Christina convinced me to take off my shoe.

I gingerly removed the shoe from my foot and said, "Hey! I think there really is something inside my shoe." I reached my hand into the shoe, and to my amazement, I discovered a pair of socks stuffed deep in the toe of my shoe! Apparently, in packing for our trip, I had put the socks inside my shoes and had forgotten to take them out. How could I have missed something so obvious?

Christina burst out laughing when she saw the socks. "Why didn't you take off your shoe four hours ago?" she asked through her giggles. We both laughed all the way through the next swim event, with Gene giving us dirty looks the entire time.

Don't let the little irritations of life keep you from enjoying the moment. I walked around in pain for more than four hours because I refused to address the real problem. Some people walk around for four years, or four decades, with an irritant rankling in their hearts or minds, and it makes them miserable. Take quick steps to alleviate any bitterness or resentment or other irritations. They don't get better with time; they simply make your life more miserable. As we age, anyone can become cynical. But you don't have to. Watch out for those little foxes that can destroy the entire field. Life is too short to let the little things get to you.

Okay, so you are getting older. So what? It beats the alternatives! Have patience with yourself and a generosity of spirit with others, and always keep your zest for life.

# CHAPTER THIRTEEN

# HELP OTHERS GO BEYOND WHERE YOU HAVE GONE.

C ertainly, we all have a responsibility to give back, to appreciate the sacrifices our forefathers have made, and to be diligent in helping others enjoy those same freedoms and opportunities. Even more important than giving back to society, however, is a determination to "pay it forward," to help others go beyond where you have gone. This is one of the key motivations of life at my age.

Why am I alive? What am I supposed to do before I die? These are questions everyone should ask, not just octogenarians such as me. At any age, you will be more excited and more effective when you are motivated and activated by the desire to fulfill the purpose you believe you were born to do.

Whatever path your life takes, find time and a way to give something back; give time, talent, or treasure to help your community, or to help someone else achieve his or her goal. Look beyond the mirror where you see only yourself, and see a world with millions of people whose lives you might impact positively, or more important, find one person in whose life you can help make a positive difference. Reaching out and helping another person will bring you more satisfaction than anything you have ever done.

Learn to ask, "How can I help you? What can I offer you?"

That's what ignites my rockets to this day. Every day I wake up and begin working on some way to help motivate the next generation to develop a challenging but realistic goal of exploring space. So I kicked up some dust on the Moon. Big deal. That was great, but I don't want that to be my only legacy. I don't want to be remembered as an iconic voice from the past; I want to be remembered for making a huge impact on the future! I won't be around to see it, but I want to lay the groundwork for the next generation of explorers.

Nowadays, I consider myself a global statesman for space and have been doing my part to try and move our space program forward.

One of my goals yet to be achieved is to see all 24 of the astronauts—living or deceased—who reached the Moon, including the 12 who landed on the surface, designated as Lunar Ambassadors. In the meantime, I continue my efforts as a global space statesman.

In 1985, I started the ShareSpace Foundation to lobby for a lottery to give regular, everyday people a chance to travel into space, so it wouldn't be something only governments and the rich folks can do. At first, some people thought my suggestions were the stuff of science fiction, but now with companies like Virgin Galactic, XCOR, and Blue Origin, space tourism is becoming reality. I have no doubt that everyday people will soon start taking suborbital flights. I'm also the AXE Apollo Space Ambassador, and they recently gave away 22 suborbital flights to winners from all over the world, so I'm excited to see my dream of space tourism come to fruition.

But my main focus is Mars! I participated with great honor in America's initial landing on the Moon, and now I am devoting my life to encouraging and enabling Americans to lead the way in an international effort to land on Mars and establish a permanent presence there. Returning to the Moon with NASA astronauts is not the best use of our resources. Instead, we need to direct our efforts to go beyond the Moon, to establish habitation and laboratories on the surface of Mars.

I have always felt Mars should be the next destination following our landings on the Moon. I've been vocal about it for a long time, and the dream of reaching Mars is finally getting closer to becoming a reality. With the Curiosity rover now on the surface of Mars and showing us more sights than ever before, I'm hoping it will pique the curiosity of young people and motivate them to explore beyond Earth and the Moon and on to Mars.

Human settlement on Mars is possible today with existing technologies. Components are well tested and readily available from industry leaders worldwide. The first footprints on Mars and the lives of the crew will captivate and inspire future generations, but I'm convinced that we should develop a colony on Mars, a permanent settlement, not just a landing area. Permanence is the key, right from the get-go. Some of my colleagues don't feel that establishing a settlement on Mars is wise; others consider it a suicide mission. I disagree. Over a period of six or seven years, we can construct a habitat and laboratory on Mars. Certainly, some people will go to Mars, stay for a while, and return to Earth, but we should also seek out and encourage people who wish to travel to Mars and remain there for the rest of their lives.

Did the Pilgrims on the *Mayflower* sit around Plymouth Rock waiting for a return ship to England? Absolutely not! They traveled to the New World to settle. And that's what I hope we will be doing on Mars. When you go to Mars, you need to have made the decision that you're there permanently. The more people we have there, the more it can become a sustainable environment. Except for very rare exceptions, the people who go to Mars shouldn't be coming back. Once you get on the surface, you're there, helping to build a colony.

On the Big Island of Hawaii, some of these ideas are currently being tested, and scientists as well as volunteers are simulating life on Mars. On a portion of the island that looks very similar to the terrain of Mars, people are learning how to live on Mars. They are practicing how to function through the use of robots and rovers, remotely controlled and manipulated by satellite from a safe location, and learning how to dock various pieces of equipment on uneven terrains—even docking habitats in which more people can live. The colonization of Mars is getting closer every day!

That's why I was excited when Christina gave me several T-shirts with slogans saying something about Mars. She found a shirt that said "Mars Today" and another that said "Occupy Mars," and then she showed me one with the slogan "Get Your Ass to Mars." I thought, *That's it! That's for me! I love it!* Actually, as much as I use the phrase, I cannot take credit for it. Christina saw it initially on a shirt advertising the movie *Total Recall*. I realized that some people might be offended if they saw me wearing such a shirt, but I also knew it would be a great way to call attention to my goal of motivating people to go to Mars.

The first time I wore the shirt, we were in Dubai, getting ready to board a plane, and Christina took a picture and sent it out on Twitter. I was wearing a red flight suit and did a "Superman" pose. The picture went around the world!

I started wearing the shirt everywhere I went, and before long, other people were asking, "Hey, Buzz, where can I get one of those shirts?" So we designed our own, and now people everywhere are wearing the GYATM shirts. Anything that causes people to pay attention and helps keep the focus on the mission to Mars is fine with me! And all sorts of people wanted to wear one. Before long, I spotted people everywhere wearing "Get Your Ass to Mars" shirts, from Dave Grohl of the Foo Fighters to Jim Lovell of Apollo 13 fame. And they looked good!

The GYATM campaign took off like a Saturn rocket. I began receiving invitations for speaking engagements that went something like this: "Dear Mr. Aldrin, Please Get Your Ass to Korea and tell us how we can get to Mars." So I plan to get my ass to Korea, to Australia, and to anywhere else an opportunity comes up to encourage people that we can do it. We *can* get our collective ass to Mars!

(

ALTHOUGH I AM APPRECIATIVE and supportive of the commercial ventures now pursuing space travel, and I understand why some people feel the private sector should lead the way to Mars, I disagree that governments of nations should not be involved. This monumental achievement by humanity should not be done by one private company. It should be accomplished by a collection of the best from all the countries on Earth, and in the same way that we remember President Kennedy's challenge that motivated us to dream of reaching the Moon, the leader of the nation who makes a commitment to land on Mars within two decades will be remembered throughout history.

Obviously, I am passionate about forging our future in space. People ask me all the time, "Why do we need to go to Mars?" or "Why do we even need a space program?"

Perhaps the best reason is that by venturing into space, we improve life for everyone here on Earth. The scientific advancements and innovations that come from this type of research create products and technology that we use in our daily lives, and provide even more convenience to people all over the world every day. For example, the technology and the satellites used for communications by cell phones, GPS, and

most television networks have been possible because of invest-
ments in the space program.

Space activities provide shared experiences for people of
diverse countries and can promote cultural acceptance, expand
international cooperation, and reduce social gaps. Indirectly,
the exploration of space can encourage peace on Earth.

During the 1960s and 1970s, when the United States and
the Soviet Union engaged as adversaries in the cold war, the
competition between the two countries to achieve dominance
in space stimulated America to improve our technologies and
scientific studies. That demonstration of perseverance, along
with the dedication of our citizens and the depth of the U.S.
industrial capabilities, went a long way toward convincing
Soviet premier Mikhail Gorbachev that his nation could not
match our potential. The announcement by President Ronald
Reagan that we would develop a strategic defense initiative,
dubbed "Star Wars" by the program's detractors, was a major
factor in ending the cold war. So in a way, America's pursuit of
space exploration brought peace to our country and reduced
the threat of nuclear war worldwide.

Although I have spent most of my life distrusting the Soviet
Union, one of the truly marvelous accomplishments of the
space program was the cooperative effort in which the United
States worked together with the Soviets in 1975 to dock our
Apollo spacecraft with the Soyuz spacecraft. Think of that: In
the midst of the cold war, our two nations found it expedient
to work together in a peaceful effort. It just goes to show what
*could* happen if we allowed the exploration of space to draw us

together rather than exaggerating our differences and driving us into another expensive and counterproductive space race.

Occasionally, someone will ask me, "Buzz, why do you encourage space cooperation with Russia and China? You know we can't trust those guys." Truth is, we have little choice right now, but despite our cautions, I am hopeful that our nations can move into deep space exploration, cooperating above the atmosphere for peaceful purposes.

Nevertheless, as in many spheres of life, an important safeguard is to respect power but always be suspicious of it. We need to keep that principle in mind when working together with nations such as Russia and China. The old adage "Keep your friends close and your enemies closer" applies. For example, we must respect China's power and capabilities, while always being suspicious of its methods and motivations. The Chinese are not America's enemies, but they are not exactly our friends, either. They are well known for their attempts to hack into our nation's computer systems and for their devious efforts to obtain any technological advantage possible over the United States. To dismiss that with a wave of the hand would be a mistake.

At the same time, China has become a world power and a major player in space, and we would be silly to ignore the potential exploration we could pursue by cooperation. China has copied the older Russian space technology and has far surpassed it.

Regardless of what the Russians or the Chinese do, America needs a revival of that sort of emphasis today, developing our technology and placing a big goal in front of our country, especially for our youth, a goal large enough to inspire our nation to pursue excellence and greatness rather than mediocrity.

A good education is essential. That is why I stress the importance of STEAM—Science, Technology, Engineering, Arts, and Math—as key elements in the successes of my career. When I was in the Apollo program, the United States led the world in STEAM subjects. And that was a big part of why we did so well with the space program. Today, we have a great need for improvement in these studies. Many students complete an entire college education without even taking introductory classes in these vital subjects. But if you ever hope to explore space, you must first explore some STEAM classes. Besides, every country needs a strong STEAM workforce tailored to its specific economic, social, and cultural situation. We cannot just do space stuff for geeks; we need to explore STEAM classes for the benefit of every human being.

I also encourage undergraduate aerospace engineering students to enroll in flight classes. As you experience the joy of flying and the freedom of soaring through the air, and as you study the mechanics of how flight is possible—the laws of motion and how air can provide lift when it is moved by propulsion, causing an airplane to defy gravity as it is in the sky, and then safely returning to the Earth—I hope you will become as passionate about the possibilities of space travel as I am—or more!

(

On August 25, 2012, I received a call from Christina, sharing information with me that I really didn't want to hear. "Buzz, Neil Armstrong passed away today. Some sort of complications due to heart surgery."

I felt as though someone had let all the air out of my lungs. "Oh, no," I sighed. Neil was 82 years old, and I had really hoped that he and I would live long enough to celebrate together the 50th anniversary of our landing on the Moon in 2019. "I really thought that we could make it, that the three of us, Neil, Mike, and I, could celebrate that big anniversary together," I told Christina. Neil's death saddened me as much as if he were a member of my own family.

My daughter, Jan, and I attended the private ceremony honoring Neil in his hometown, and Christina and I attended the service in honor of Neil at the Washington National Cathedral. The cavernous cathedral was filled to capacity with family, NASA dignitaries, and many Navy cadets sitting in honor of one of their own. Christina and I sat in the front row, just off the pulpit area, along with John Glenn and his wife, and Diana Krall, who later sang "Fly Me to the Moon." Mike Collins had a part in the ceremony, so he sat at the front of the sanctuary along with the minister. From the moment I heard the first sounds of the Scottish bagpiper walking down the majestic cathedral's center aisle, followed by the Navy honor guard, I knew it was going to be an emotionally difficult yet moving tribute to Neil. Indeed, the ceremony was somber, but not sad. As Gene Cernan, the most recent man to walk on the Moon during Apollo 17, eulogized our friend, I let my eyes wander to the National Cathedral's south-side wall, where a sensational stained glass window contained one of the rocks we brought back from the Moon. Neil would have appreciated that.

Perhaps one of the most poignant portions of the ceremony came when the recorded voice of President John F. Kennedy echoed through the hallowed hall, challenging America to land a man on the Moon before the end of the decade. Kennedy did not say anything about landing two men on the Moon, but Neil and I had done that. Nor did President Kennedy say anything in his speech about walking on the lunar surface, but Neil and I had done that as well.

Now nearly 50 years since I stepped onto the Moon, and with my colleague Neil Armstrong gone, the reality is, soon I will be gone as well—although not for a few more decades, I hope! Nevertheless, after all these years, one of the hardest questions for me to answer is: "What did it feel like to walk on the Moon?" Of course, I've tried to answer that question in various ways, but because I am a scientist rather than a poet, I've never adequately described the awesomeness of the experience. Perhaps it is impossible to do so.

Recently, a little girl asked me this very question, and I said, "Squishy," with a twinkle in my eye. She understood.

But I often answer the question by returning to the first words that came into my head after setting foot on the lunar surface and gazing around: "Magnificent. Magnificent desolation."

Although we had little time for ruminations that day as I looked out at the darkness beyond the horizon and the tiny blue marble of Earth 250,000 miles away, I was struck by the magnificence of it all—not merely the Moon's appearance, but the fact that human beings were standing on it, that *I* was stepping on surfaces that had not been disturbed in thousands of years. I was awed by the magnificence of the technology that had made my steps on the Moon possible, and by the imagination and courage of people on Earth to dream of expanding our capabilities. All that and more was wrapped up in my exclamation, "Magnificent."

Yet it was also desolate—more desolate than any place on Earth. There was no atmosphere, no plant life, no signs of life anywhere. Beyond me, I could see the surface of the Moon curving away into the horizon and the sky of black velvet sheen in every direction. It seemed so cold, colder than anything on Earth, although I knew that when the Sun came up, the lunar surface would get extremely hot. So, yes, it was magnificent, but the starkly barren, monochromatic hues all around me evoked my spontaneous expression, "Magnificent desolation." After all these years, that is still the best description I've come up with in trying to convey my first impressions and the enormity of it all.

Looking back at Earth from the Moon, a question darted across my mind: Where are the billions of people on that little marble that I'm looking at? It struck me that of all the human beings, living or dead, Neil, Mike, and I were the only three not there.

☽

CHRISTINA AND I WERE TALKING recently about my age and the fact that one of these days, I am going to die.

"Yeah, and when you do, I want to send half of your ashes to Mars," she said.

"Really? Which half?" I asked.

"Depends on what I'm mad about at that time," she quipped. "But you can be sure of this, I'm going to send *your ass* to Mars!"

(

THE OATH I TOOK AS A TEENAGE BOY—"Duty, Honor, and Service to my country"—still permeates my thoughts today. Serving my country remains my paramount passion, and I'm constantly looking for new and better ways to do it.

Besides encouraging the next generation of space explorers, another of my priorities has been to help honor and better care for our country's veterans—the men and women who have sacrificed so much so that our nation and world can live in freedom and peace. Certainly, I want to be of service to America's space program, but I also want to continue to be of service to our veterans and our military.

In October 2012, Brian Jones, an explorer in his own right who has flown around the world in a hot-air balloon, called and invited me to Great Britain to help Aerobility, a UK charity that provides flying experiences to disabled people. Their plan was to raise money by engaging more than 50 celebrities to "fly" various lengths in a realistic cockpit simulating around-the-world flights. The idea piqued my interest, so I consented to help, and we raised a ton of money for the organization.

I flew my lengths and then popped out of the simulator completely exhilarated. I loved it! "Wow, the sense of accomplishment that I feel," I said, "coming out of that cockpit . . . It is amazing."

"You?" Christina asked. "Really? After all the flying you have done, you are excited about flying in a simulator?"

"Yes, it has been a while since I've flown, or even been in a simulator, and I'd forgotten how exciting it is to me. Plus, there are a lot of things that a pilot has to concentrate on . . . You really have to focus on what you are doing . . . airspeed . . . rate of climb . . . There are all sorts of things a pilot must do." So it occurred to me that this could be a good thing for veterans who are suffering with post-traumatic stress disorder. Because one of the things they struggle with is getting out of themselves and focusing on something else besides their memories, this could be a way to help them get their minds off their problems and provide an enjoyable way to have a sense of accomplishment.

Two months later, Aerobility held the Aviators Ball, an event honoring individuals and groups connected to their cause. For instance, they gave an award to a man who has cerebral palsy and who learned to fly. Another man, wheelchair bound, learned to fly using special instrument panel adjustments, similar to those that some handicapped individuals use to drive an automobile.

When my turn came to address the crowd, I made a spontaneous, public commitment. "I have made a decision that I want to do what you are doing, but I want to focus on veterans in the United States." There it was: I was on record.

I decided to call our organization U.S. Aerobility and to focus our efforts on creating opportunities for U.S. veterans, especially those with physical disabilities, so they can learn to fly. This organization has become near and dear to my heart.

We have already provided several combat veterans who are dealing with PTSD the opportunities to fly in a simulator, and then to fly in an actual plane. It takes concentration to fly, so when the vets discover that they can focus again, it opens whole new vistas of opportunity for them. *If I can fly an airplane, what else can I do?* they wonder.

In addition to U.S. Aerobility, I have been actively involved in raising awareness for veterans in another way. Until recently, when the national anthem was being played, the military hand salute was restricted to those in active service. In 2008, though, President George W. Bush signed a bill into law allowing veterans also to hand salute the flag, rather than simply putting a hand over the heart. It is a great way that other people can take note of and appreciate the veterans who have served our country.

To help create awareness of this new practice, I created an organization called VetSalute.org and have been attending more sporting events than ever before in my life! I've been to a Los Angeles Dodgers game on Memorial Day and to an Angels game on another occasion, and when "The Star-Spangled Banner" is played, I raise my hand in salute of our flag.

Somebody said to me, "Why are you doing a hand salute, Buzz? You're not active military."

"Because I am a U.S. veteran."

"But I didn't think veterans were supposed to hand salute?"

"Oh, yes, now we can," I said.

To me, anyone who has served our country is worthy of honor, and this is simply another way that I can use my celebrity to help others go beyond where I have gone. Doing something bigger than yourself will bring you more satisfaction than all the accolades you can accumulate in life.

( 

PERHAPS MY GREATEST LEGACY WILL BE my efforts to establish USSE—United Strategic Space Enterprise—a group of international expert advisers, a nonpartisan "think tank" whose members will meet regularly to study space policy, confer, and offer their expertise to all nations pursuing the exploration of space. Of course, the idea of the U.S.S. *Enterprise* reminds many people of *Star Trek,* so I tell them that we are going to have Star Fleet Captains, led by the Star Fleet Admiral—me!

I am also passionate about working with the Buzz Aldrin Space Institute at the Florida Institute of Technology, in partnership with Purdue University, to enhance and promote my vision of Mars exploration.

Just as the United States helped win two World Wars, as well as the cold war, America can now lead the way in the peaceful exploration of space. Neil and I left a plaque on the Moon that reads, "We came in peace for all mankind." I still believe that is true, and it is the only way to effectively muster the resources—financial, intellectual, and technological—to explore deep space. Rather than competing with the Chinese or the Russians or the Italians or anyone else for dominance in space, we would be wiser to cooperate and win great victories for all nations.

As for the future, I strongly feel that we need to get the world excited again about space exploration and have the pioneering spirit to reach beyond our boundaries and current capabilities. I hope we can get the next generation to feel as we did back when I was privileged to be a part of the Apollo program.

Since our return to Earth and our splashdown in the Pacific, I've come to realize that more than the rocks we brought back or the experiments we left, the true value of Apollo 11 and the first landing on the Moon is the amazing story of innovation and teamwork that went into overcoming the obstacles to accomplish our goal.

In all, a team of 400,000 people worked together on a common dream. From the engineers, technicians, and rocket scientists who designed and built the multistage Saturn V rocket to the aerospace industry contractors, NASA administrators, and even the seamstress who sewed our space suits—it took a unified effort to accomplish everything that was needed to reach and land on the Moon.

Occasionally, someone in their teens or 20s will come up to me and say, "My grandfather worked on some of the technology for Apollo 11. Did you know him?"

Usually, I didn't. So many dedicated people worked together toward the common goal of reaching the Moon, in various locations around the country, that it was impossible for me to meet all of them. But every person's contribution to the team—regardless how large or small—mattered in the unified effort toward accomplishing the end result. The success of Apollo 11 was definitely due to a great team effort.

That effort was driven in part by competition and in part by a universal thirst for knowledge through scientific discovery. People all over the world felt they had participated in our incredible journey, as we landed and walked on another celestial body for the first time. And that feeling of participation brought together humanity, and it still holds immeasurable value and hope for future cooperation between people of all nations.

The world welcomed us back from the Moon as heroes, cheering wildly as we participated in parades and celebrations. I understood, however, that people were not simply cheering for three guys, but for what we represented—that by a lot of people working together for a common cause, we had accomplished the impossible.

(

THESE ARE A FEW OF MY FAVORITE life lessons that I learned as a result of walking on the Moon and the preparation that took us there—the guiding principles that have helped keep me going since returning to Earth.

- The sky is *not* the limit . . . there are footprints on the Moon!
- Keep your mind open to possibilities.
- Show me your friends, and I will show you your future.
- Second comes right after first.
- Write your own epitaph.
- Maintain your spirit of adventure.
- Failure is always an option.
- Practice respect for all people.
- Do what you believe is right even when others choose otherwise.
- Trust your gut . . . and your instruments.
- Laugh . . . a lot!
- Keep a young mind-set at every age.
- Help others go beyond where you have gone.

I hope these lessons will be as helpful to you as they have been to me.

Take it from a man who has walked on the Moon: Be careful what you dream—it just might come to pass, so be prepared. Apollo is the story of people at their best, working together for a common goal. We started with a dream, and we can do these kinds of things again.

With a united effort and a great team, you *too* can achieve great things. I know, because I am living proof that no dream is too high!

# ACKNOWLEDGMENTS

I 'd like to thank my family, and especially my three kids —
James Michael; my beautiful daughter, Jan; and my young-
est, Andy, who is carrying on the aerospace tradition and
my legacy. I'm still learning about what it means to be a father
and the love that close family brings. I lost both my sisters, and
each loss reminds me how much family matters. I'd like to
thank my only grandson, Jeffrey Schuss, who has done everything right. He is a good kid who became an aerospace engineer
and a pilot, and, best of all, he married April, which may be his
smartest move. They're continuing the family line with my
great-grandsons, Nathanial and Benjamin, with baby Archer
on the way. I'm grateful that both Jan and Andy married up to
smart, good-looking, funny, and sensible spouses who always
help with the non-Aldrin perspective: Bruce Hanifan and
Maureen Aldrin.

I would be lost without my team: My Mission Director,
Christina Korp, whom I consider my indispensable crutch,
holding my world up and together—and all the while travel

agenting, baggage lifting, mascot raising, keyboard pecking, ballad singing . . . and tweeting like a professional about all things Buzz. And my assistant, Rob Varnas, who keeps our gadgets in check, my website running smoothly, while at the same time photo and video archiving, Mexican food cooking, and making sure I have enough spectacles to read all the emails that come into all my devices. My mascots, Brielle Winona Korp and Logan Alexander BUZZ Korp. They represent Generation Mars.

I'd like to thank the Purdue team, who have been instrumental in helping get my concepts for Cycling Pathways to Occupy Mars out to the world, especially professor Jim Longuski, who has been a believer longer than anyone else other than me, and Ph.D. project manager Sarag Saikia.

Thank you to my committed partner and co-pilot in life, Judy Rice. You're the best person to watch sunrises with on the beach.

Thanks to all those on my National Geographic Books team: designers Nicole Miller, Melissa Farris, and Jono Halling; photographers and photo editors Becky Hale, Mark Thiessen, and Susan Blair; and production editor Michael O'Connor.

Finally, I'd like to thank my co-writer, Ken Abraham, who has helped me capture more Buzz tales to show the world another part of me, and our editor extraordinaire, Susan Tyler Hitchcock.

I hope you like this book and these stories. I've already had quite a life, but you ain't seen nothing yet!

— *BUZZ*

## ILLUSTRATIONS CREDITS

All photographs used by permission from the Buzz Aldrin Photo Archive, except the following. Photographs identified by insert page number.

Jamie Noguchi: Front cover
Rebecca Hale/National Geographic: Back cover

Linn LeBlanc: 10 (UP)
Andrew Aldrin: 10 (LO)
Christina Korp: 11 (LO LE), 12 (UP), 12 (LO), 13 (LO), 14, 15
James O. Davies: 16

# JOIN BUZZ ALDRIN
## in his inspiring and thought-provoking
# MISSION TO MARS

"Buzz Aldrin has been as far from Earth as any human being, and now he's leading the charge to go much farther, to our next epic destination: Mars."
—JAMES CAMERON

Can astronauts reach Mars by 2035? Absolutely, says Buzz Aldrin. It is not only possible, but vital to America's future to keep pushing the space frontier outward for the sake of exploration, science, development, commerce, and security.

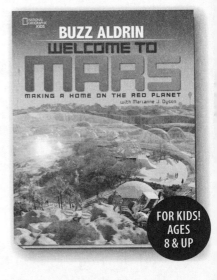

Buzz Aldrin challenges curious kids to think about Mars as not just a faraway red planet but as a possible future home for Earthlings! Find out what life might be like far, far from Earth as kids navigate their way through this fun and fascinating book.

**FOR KIDS! AGES 8 & UP**